What people are saying about *Building a Church*

Our church's rapid growth rate was overwhelming; I reached out to Dr. Porter King as a 911 to help us organize our leadership. Many of the organizational strategies used in this book were implemented. Our very first org chart was developed, helping us to train the leaders within our four walls and allowing me to focus on the overall mission of our organization instead of the pressures of growth. This is a blessing.

Pastor John F. Hannah
Senior Pastor, New Life Covenant SE

In the cultivation of congregations, wise leadership is about vigilance as well as vision. For pastors aspiring to this kind of leadership, this book is the next best thing to the Spirit-led, in-person, on-site inspiration Jeanne Porter King offers in her teaching and consulting. Not only biblically grounded but also congregational context-oriented and culturally attentive, this timely resource provides tools for the kind of pastoral paying attention essential to nurturing individuals as well as communities of believers. Insight-generating questions and strategic plan-producing worksheets will enable the tailoring of day-to-day and year-to-year practices of leadership for churches seeking to live out their vocation as a priesthood of all believers.

Dr. Virstan Choy
Director of Advanced Pastoral Studies
San Francisco Theological Seminary

Building a Church Full of Leaders is essential reading for pastors who want to harness the full leadership potential within their churches. The leadership capacity crisis is one of the most serious threats to the longevity of the institutional church and the entire non-profit sector in the twenty-first century. This handbook blends timeless scriptural truths and management insights to equip leaders to tackle the challenge head on. Every pastor and leader should make it their business to develop and deploy a church full of leaders.

Rev. Nicholas Pearce, Ph.D.
Clinical Assistant Professor of Management & Organizations
Kellogg School of Management, Northwestern University

Building a Church Full of Leaders provides more than theory; it provides necessary application. The book engages church leaders, no matter the size of their congregation, by maintaining a sensitivity to the leadership development that must take place as church populations change. The author lays out an important structure and system for a church's success in this critical area of development: a feat that can only be described as exemplary. Readers will be struck by the transformative nature of each chapter; Dr. Porter King is always mindful of process, growth, and the ever-present next step. This book is a must read for pastors in particular and church leaders in general.

Bishop Howard Tillman
Pastor, New Covenant Believer's Church, Columbus, Ohio

Dr. Porter King's work as a church consultant has been invaluable to Oakdale Covenant Church of Chicago. Naturally, the congregation expects the pastor and a few seasoned parishioners to lead the congregation, but if we expect success, it is essential to include as many parishioners as possible. Dr. Porter King's Church Full of Leaders (CFOL) system is an innovative resource that fosters the leadership skills of the entire church body. Church Full of Leaders (CFOL) has given us a larger talent pool to draw from for various leadership positions and opportunities in our congregation and community. Our leadership has been revitalized and our vision has been sharpened. This book is a must read for any and all pastors that are serious about developing their entire congregation into a church full of leaders.

Dr. D. Darrell Griffin, D.Min.
Senior Pastor, Oakdale Covenant Church of Chicago

This book recognizes the value and potential of the entire congregation and provides tangible tools for developing leaders at all levels. Biblically sound leadership principles form the framework for growth and development. An emphasis on transformative leadership serves to generate a servant's heart that leads out of relationship with Jesus and not duty. This is kingdom building at a foundational level. Most importantly for me as a pastor, this book is designed to aid pastors of small and medium-sized churches. Many excellent books on leadership development require a leadership structure to be somewhat in place. This book can help pastors start their ministry from ground zero while also helping small, established ministries re-energize and focus on developing different levels of leaders. It's not a one size fits all—it is a much-needed tool to help build a church full of leaders.

Pastor Elaine Graham
God's Word Christian Center

Every pastor would love to have Dr. Porter King on his or her staff managing leadership development and systems management. Obviously, that is not possible. What is possible, and what I strongly recommend, is to take Dr. Porter King's labor of love, *Building a Church Full of Leaders* book/training manual/roadmap to church growth and maturation, to your churches, your organizations, or your own home. Read it, meditate on it, and most of all implement it in your ministry. By the way, I am taking my own advice. *Building a Church Full of Leaders* by Dr. Jeanne Porter King is now my favorite leadership development and systems manual. You will do well to make it yours as well.

Bishop Clifford L. Frazier
Co-Founder of the Battle For The Family &
Senior Pastor of The Sanctuary Family Church

Building a Church Full of Leaders is a must read for any pastor of ministry team leaders serious about investing in the human capital that resides within their pews. My first ministerial assignment was in a church whose ethos was social justice and racial equality; therefore, leading in a multicultural environment/society was central to our core values. Dr. Porter King was sought out early on to facilitate the kind of leadership training that would develop our staff and ministry teams in a systematic process of spiritual formation, strategic organizing, and skill building. As an executive pastor today, my leadership toolbox would be deficient without the transformative tools provided in this book.

Randall K. Blakey, Executive Pastor, LaSalle Street Church
President, Near North Ministry Alliance, Chicago, Illinois

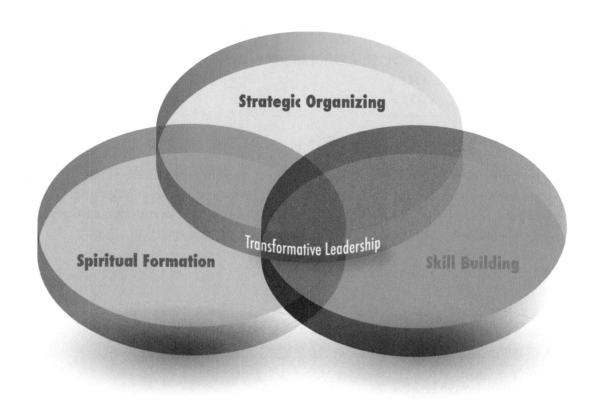

Building a Church
FULL OF Leaders

A GUIDE FOR UNLEASHING THE LEADERSHIP POTENTIAL OF YOUR CHURCH

Jeanne Porter King

TRANSPORTER COMMMUNICATION LLC

LIFE TO LEGACY, LLC
www.life2legacy.com

© 2014 by Jeanne Porter King

Published by TransPorter Commmunication LLC
430 E 162nd Street, #441
South Holland, IL 60473

Printed in the United States of America

Library of Congress Control Number: 2014937233

King, Jeanne Porter
Church Full of Leaders: Unleashing the Leadership Potential of Your Church

ISBN: 978-1-939654-21-2

1. Church leadership. 2. Lay leadership. 3. Transformative leadership

www.life2legacy.com

Contents

Foreword

In 2011 the Lord laid on my heart to identify and train more leaders in the church where I serve as pastor. We were at the threshold of a new level of growth, and the Lord was letting me know that developing leaders would be key to crossing that threshold. At that time, little did I know that later that year I would meet Dr. Jeanne Porter, such an insightful and skilled leadership developer, and God would join us in matrimony and ministry partnership the next year.

Over the past year we have been using the concepts and frameworks in this book to build our own Church Full of Leaders. Ministry cannot be accomplished by the solitary pastor. As a third generation pastor in the Church of God in Christ, a district superintendent, and the Dean of the Institute for the National Pastors and Elders Conference, I have a heart for pastors and am intimately aware of the tasks and challenges of pastoral leadership.

Whether urban or suburban, the contexts for ministry have become more complex. Our surrounding communities are riddled with violence, under employment, economic disparity, and educational crises. Pastors are stressed grappling with preaching, teaching, pastoral cares, budget management, and program development. Yet we believe that the church is a haven of spiritual vitality for people young and old. Though challenging, the joys of ministry can be great.

The pastor cannot do it alone; however, *Building a Church Full of Leaders* is a valuable tool for pastors. It provides strategy and structure for developing a culture of leadership in which more and more of the congregation can be enjoined and engaged in the work of ministry. According to Ephesians 4:11-12, our charge is to equip and train the people of God for the work of ministry. *Building a Church Full of Leaders* is a timely resource for doing just that.

As a pastor I can speak to other pastors about the importance of leadership and developing competent men and women of character to bring a God-given vision for a church to fruition. As a national institute director I can speak to pastors about the necessity of staying abreast of relevant tools. Dr. Jeanne Porter King has brought it together in one volume to help pastors develop more leaders and enhance the effectiveness of their churches.

Rev. Dr. Carl E. King Sr.
Pastor, Christ Community Church, South Holland, Illinois
Dean of the Institute for the Pastors and Elders Conference
Church of God in Christ, Inc.

Acknowledgments

This book has been over twenty years in the making. From the time I was first working on a doctorate in organizational behavior at The Ohio State University, I remember standing on the steps of the building that housed the business school declaring to a friend from church, "I want to use organizational behavior principles to build stronger churches." Well, I didn't complete my doctorate at that school; but as God would have it, the Lord led me into a career of consulting that was to last a lifetime. I eventually entered a doctoral program where, instead of focusing just on business organizations, I studied all types of organizational systems, including churches. In this program, I focused on the development of leaders, especially as it relates to communities of color. I ultimately completed seminary to flesh out the theological underpinnings of all my work, including leadership spirituality. But don't worry—this book is not intended to be a theological or philosophical treatise.

This book is anchored in twenty years of practical hands-on work in churches of all sizes, from small to medium, to large to mega. I have been blessed to consult in a range of church systems as well as to serve on staff in as diverse a range of churches.

For a number of years I developed leadership programs for churches, and one such church was the Faith Community of St. Sabina, pastored by Rev. Michael Pfleger. I received a call from him one day and he said, "Dr. Porter, I want to build a church full of leaders," and from there I embarked upon a nearly six-year journey with his church, developing the frameworks and curriculum that ultimately trained some 300 leaders. The lessons learned about equipping members of the congregation with leadership skills so that we truly cultivate a church full of leaders stayed with me and served as the guiding vision for my future leadership consulting and, obviously, the title of this book.

I have been blessed to work with churches from the East Coast to the West Coast, and numerous cities in between, but two other engagements are noteworthy. In 1995, upon completion of my doctoral program, I had relocated to Chicago for a faculty appointment at a local university. For a variety of reasons, I stayed at this school a mere five quarters, but during that time developed what would become a seventeen-year relationship with a mega church in the Woodlawn neighborhood of Chicago under the pastorate of Bishop Arthur M. Brazier. "Bishop," as we fondly called him, became my pastor and also my mentor, a model of pastoral leadership. In 1995, as a newly minted Ph.D., the first project Bishop asked me to work on was with his son, the then church administrator, Elder Byron Brazier. Our task was to develop a new model of leadership for the rapidly growing church. At the Apostolic Church of God, I continued to develop leadership programs and processes for hundreds of leaders over the next ten years or so. Upon Bishop's retirement in 2008, I joined the pastoral staff of the

Apostolic Church of God under his successor, Dr. Brazier, leading the ministry and leadership development processes. It was an ideal position for one called to develop church leaders.

In 2012, I married a visionary pastor and joined him in ministry in south suburban Chicago. I have been blessed to bring twenty plus years of leadership development practice to our bustling community church. I now serve as the executive pastor for Christ Community Church, and again I serve in an ideal position. I asked my husband, Dr. Carl King Sr., to write the foreword because many of the ideas in this book were refined at Christ Community, as he follows a God-given vision for community-based ministry, and he and I together develop the leaders of our church. He has helped to make the material far more practical and accessible, and I am grateful for his incisive, keen eye.

So many people influenced my thinking and practice of leadership, too many to note here. But three are especially noteworthy. Special thanks go to Jennifer LuVert of Forerunners Ink. Her quality and excellence in layout and publishing cannot be surpassed. I want to acknowledge Steven Holman-Robinson, who served as our summer intern at Christ Community Church last summer and compiled the Glossary of Technology Apps for Communication and Meetings. We were blessed to have Steven serve in our ministry.

Since 2008, I have been blessed to teach the Fundamentals of Leadership for Certificate in Executive Leadership at McCormick Theological Seminary. This course has enabled me to further refine my thinking on pastoral leadership with the pastors who have come from a wide variety of denominations. Many thanks go to Jeff Japinga, Assistant Dean of the DMin and Certificate programs, for continuing to lead and support the faculty of the Certificate in Executive Leadership Program (CELP). To the many CELP pastors who asked for this book—thank you for joining me at some juncture on this journey. Finally, I thank the leaders of Christ Community Church, to whom I dedicate this book.

So as you see, this handbook is the outcome of over two decades of praxis—leadership practice informed by prayerful, diligent theological reflection that further guides practice. It has been a journey of careful and consistent working through of leadership frameworks, models, principles, and practices that I now offer to pastors wanting to cultivate a leadership culture in their churches. This book is aimed at the small to medium-sized church. In my experience, these churches are the ones that need guidance in getting an infrastructure built upon which to grow to the next level, yet these churches are the ones in which pastors are stretched, under-resourced, and in need of processes to galvanize more of the congregation into leadership.

Acknowledgments

May *Building a Church Full of Leaders* inspire pastors to continue to unleash the leadership potential in their churches and provide guidance, wisdom, and processes for growing leaders at every level of the church.

Dr. Jeanne Porter King

Transformative Leadership: A Framework for Church Leaders

1

If you've taken the time to open or download this book, then I'm sure you're serious about investing in the people of your congregation and building a leadership culture that moves your church forward. This handbook was written to help pastors of small to medium-sized churches develop a comprehensive leadership infrastructure and culture. The reality is we need to develop more spiritually mature, strategically organized, skilled leaders for our churches—especially small to medium-sized churches where engaging more people into ministry is critical to both church growth and member growth, as well as to pastoral longevity.

God has sent to our churches people with gifts and potential that too often sit in the pew on Sunday but are not involved in the life of the church—sometimes they don't see a place for them to serve or sometimes they have not been challenged to step up. Yet in most churches I know of, current leaders are overextended and underdeveloped.

Think of the people in your congregation who have excellent leadership skills—they are faithful and dependable, they follow through, they manage ministry projects well, and they motivate others to participate in ministry. Who are these people? What percentage of the congregation do they represent? They probably don't make up a large percentage of your congregation. So let's dig deeper.

You have more leadership potential in your congregation than you realize. Think of additional people who faithfully attend worship services and occasionally attend ministry events for their affinity group—women, men, singles, married couples, teens. Think of the people who attend your church and are active in the community. These people represent a level of leadership potential you probably have not tapped. But you can dig deeper.

Think of the business people, the educators, the agency directors, and the public servants who attend your church. They have an opportunity to influence policy and practices that shape the quality of life for the people of your community. These people comprise another type and level of leadership potential. But you can still dig deeper!

Now think about the "ordinary" Joe and Jane that seem to have no special gifts or calling; they are faithful, yet they make no fanfare. They too represent an un-mined field of potential that can be harnessed and unleashed to increase the overall leadership capacity of your church.

The first step in building a Church Full of Leaders is for you, the pastor, head of staff, or member of pastoral staff to revise your notion of a leader. Change the image or faces of those you assume to be leaders. If you can believe that God has gifted every member of your congregation in some way, then perhaps you can imagine each of those members offering their gifts in the service and leadership processes of your church. The key will be for you to define leadership, distinguish what it means to be a leader in the church, develop a statement of your church's vision and mission, and identify how increasing the leadership capacity will help to serve the vision and mission. Then you will need to organize a method and structure for training and developing leaders, and delivering ministry in which more people are involved in serving.

This handbook, *Building a Church Full of Leaders*, will help you do just that—put together a development and delivery system for increasing your leadership capacity. The Church Full of Leaders (Church Full of Leaders) process comprises three essential functions, or components, for developing transformative leaders:

- a strategic leadership function to plan and organize for transformative ministry
- a spiritual formation component to promote the leaders' spiritual growth and personal transformation
- a skill-building component to equip leaders with tools and competencies to lead transformatively

The Church Full of Leaders process entails in-depth planning by the pastor and head of staff to set the tone, direction, and expectations for leadership. In addition, it provides a framework for training and developing current and future leaders. This book is designed to assist the pastor, pastoral staff, board of trustees, and/or advisory board in thinking through your current context of ministry and identifying the type and extent of leadership development that will help you fulfill the church's vision. The chapters of this manual can also be adapted in order to train leaders in your congregation. The modules are designed to provide a curriculum for systematically and consistently training leaders of your church on core leadership principles and practices.

How to Use This Book

Building a Church Full of Leaders is an informative, intensive, and interactive guide for developing a systematic leadership training process that will ignite leadership embers within your church. The following suggestions will help you optimize the use of this handbook:

- Form a leadership team to pray about, study, and explore the leadership processes delineated in this manual. Too often, pastors attempt to accomplish great works in their church by themselves. The message of *Building a Church Full of Leaders* is that pastors need other leaders to fulfill the ministry mission and vision of their church. Enlist the

leadership power of your church from the very beginning of this leadership development process; thus, model how your leaders are to enlist other leaders into their ministries and auxiliary processes.

- Use *Building a Church Full of Leaders* as a workbook. Read the chapters, answer the questions, and complete the activities. The first section of the book, Strategic Organizing,will help you clarify the processes and activities that will be necessary to engage the leaders of your church. The completed activities will help you develop handouts and forms that will be used in the Church Full of Leaders development process. These documents will provide the leaders of your church with the shared vision, clear expectations, and common language they will need to become leaders who will move your church forward. The second section, Spiritual Formation, and third section, Skill Building, can be used to directly develop ministry leaders. These have been written with ministry leaders in mind, with reflection questions that will help both pastor and ministry leader.

- Get started today. Don't delay. It is time to unleash the potential that is within the church. It is time to prepare God's people for works of service and to help them understand their role in fulfilling the mission of the church. It is time to build churches where the gifts of the people of God are recognized, offered, accepted, and utilized. It is time to build a Church Full of Leaders!

Imagine a church whose members so closely identify with the gospel message that each person embraces his or her responsibility and privilege to participate in the transformation of the world. Imagine a church where members are so fully empowered by the Holy Spirit and the Word of God that they see themselves as agents of change, discerning and awaiting opportunities to bring about transformation in the conditions around them.

Such an assembly is really a Church Full of Leaders. A Church Full of Leaders is a church that sees building up, nurturing, and equipping its people for ministry within the church, as well as outside its walls, as a crucial part of its mission. In this church, every member participates in the transformative leadership processes of the church. One notable and noted pastor emeritus, when referring to the leadership practices of a particular church tradition once said, "We are some of the hardest people to follow because we think we are all leaders." Yet, in a Church Full of Leaders, all members do not lead at the same time! Ideally, however, all members do share in leading in the church; they participate in the leadership functions at every level. In a Church Full of Leaders, we each are sometimes leader, sometimes follower but always servant.

These leaders are neither ordinary members who come to church only on Sundays, nor are they people who clamor for titles and positions, but they are people of God who see spiritual leadership as an integral responsibility of discipleship. These individuals have accepted the mandate of the gospel to radically change the society around them and participate in the ushering in of the kingdom of God. This radical brand of leadership challenges the perceptions and paradigms of traditional church leaders, but it is necessary in order to mobilize our congregations toward transformative ministry in this day.

A New Model of Leadership

We are experiencing a shift in the way we understand leadership. Looking past traditional concepts of leadership, many pastors are tapping into an understanding of leadership that is inclusive of the broad membership of their congregations; they are looking to empower people to serve and offer their gifts in the attainment of the broader mission and vision of the church. They desire to equip laity and clergy with skills and tools that help them lead together. They have decided to invest in the people in the pews, so that the people in the pews can accomplish the purposes of the church. Churches that are the most effective in growing spiritually mature members who serve their communities through the love of Christ, have cultivated a leadership culture in which the core values of the church include the expectations that members are developed to participate in the leadership processes of the church; they take initiative and responsibility for ministry, and they get the work of ministry done through cultivating and catalyzing the gifts of the people of God. The core values and assumptions and language of these churches give evidence to leaders who are committed, creative, and connected.

Leadership both inside and outside of the church is a spiritual practice of integrity and accountability, as well as personal and communal transformation. Becoming a leader requires discipline, and its authentic practice can transform how we see ourselves and the world around us. Many members already assume some type of service or function within our churches. Many others see (or could be helped to see) the church as a place where they sort through and affirm within themselves spiritual values that then infuse their daily professional and personal lives, thus enabling them to enact and practice ethical leadership within their societal contexts. Consequently, churches must become more intentional in equipping members for both types of service—leading inside and outside the church.

From Traditional to Transformative Leadership

The underlying paradigm for a Church Full of Leaders is that of transformative leadership—a type of leadership in which multiple layers of leadership exist, and each layer of leadership moves the next layer to higher spiritual and moral levels. As Scripture teaches us, we spur on one another to love and good deeds (Hebrews 10:24). This movement creates a ripple effect in which more and more members are encouraged to participate in the ministries of the church, as the church continues to spread the gospel, converting souls and bringing broken people to a place of wholeness. Biblically based transformative leadership recognizes the leadership capacity in each born-again believer. Though each believer may not hold a title or position, he or she is still called to be salt and light and have a transforming influence on the society in which he or she lives. Sadly, down through the years church leaders too often have borrowed leadership models from the secular society that placed the mantle of leadership on a select few; and each wore such titles with a sense of privilege, often using the title and authority to control followers.

This traditional conception of leadership was based more on a sterile model and viewed the church as just another type of organization. Biblically based transformative leadership recognizes the church as the body of Christ—a life-giving organism in which leaders under the direction and power of the Holy Spirit help maintain the flow of the organism. Yet biblically based transformative leadership understands that every organism organizes; so transformative leaders understand the critical role of organizational leadership to the church. Leaders in a Church Full of Leaders embrace and help to build up the organism and organization that we know as the church. The chart in Figure 1 contrasts some of the differences between traditional and transformative leadership.

Figure 1: Traditional and Transformative Leadership—A Comparison

Traditional Leadership	Transformative Leadership
❏ Focuses on the individual leader (as defined by a title or position) and his or her vision, purposes, and goals	❏ Focuses on the sovereign God as leader. God chooses and places human leaders to fulfill His plans and purposes as He wills
❏ Relies solely on position in the hierarchy for identity and authority	❏ Relies on our position in Christ for identity and humbly accepts the delegated authority that comes with the position
❏ Emphasis on structure and hierarchy	❏ Emphasis on structure, process, and relationship
❏ Appeals to head knowledge	❏ Appeals to the head and the heart
❏ Can be elitist	❏ Is based on the work of grace and, therefore, is based on equality
❏ Encourages assimilation (to become like the top leader in style and substance)	❏ Encourages change and transformation (to become what God intends for you to be)
❏ Forces people to be conformed to a corporate image	❏ Encourages people to be conformed to the image of Christ
❏ Cultivates an "either-or" perspective—a person is a leader or not	❏ Cultivates a "both-and" perspective—we each are both leader and follower, depending on the time, and always servant
❏ Operates from a "secular" paradigm ▶ Planning based on the numbers ▶ Accountability by control ▶ Coordinating like functions and sameness ▶ Motivational methods that sometimes feel manipulative ▶ Profitability is the major measure for success	❏ Operates from a stewardship paradigm ▶ Praying (to receive revelation of God's plan) ▶ Mutual accountability ▶ Unity through the Holy Spirit (not false consensus) ▶ Motivational methods that inspire the people of God to serve ▶ Fruitfulness and faithfulness are measures of success

One of the aims of *Building a Church Full of Leaders* is to help more church leaders move from traditional notions of leadership to transformative leadership.

Building a Church Full of Leaders

Effecting change at many levels is a vital function of the twenty-first century church. Any pastor with a God-given vision to transform the church and surrounding community cannot accomplish such a vision alone. She or he must enlist the gifts and services of other leaders throughout the congregation,

thus building a Church Full of Leaders. The Church Full of Leaders training is a process aimed at helping the local church identify and activate its leadership capabilities.

An underlying premise of a Church Full of Leaders is that all believers have leadership capacity. Although all believers are not called to specific leadership offices or positions, every member has leadership responsibility—the ability to respond to the mandate of the gospel to meet the pressing needs and issues of the day. Some may never hold a leadership office or have the spiritual gift of leadership (Romans 12:8), but all believers can develop leadership skills that increase their effectiveness in the work of ministry.

Working with churches over the past several years to develop and build a Church Full of Leaders has helped us glean a number of lessons.

Leadership is necessary for the church and is mandated by God. *Building a Church Full of Leaders* is based on a God-ordained mandate, not on human constructions that privilege some groups of people over others. Leadership is something that, from the beginning of creation, God bestowed upon man and woman by giving them dominion over the earth. God's charge to humankind was to be responsible stewards, or trustees, of the earth and its resources (Genesis 1:27-28). This idea of leadership became perverted with the fall of humankind and evolved into domination over one another instead of dominion with each other. Instead of being God-centered, leadership became self-centered; instead of seeking to be fruitful and share the abundance, leaders began to hoard; instead of seeking the good of all, leaders created systems that protected others who were most like them. The good news is that just as humans were redeemed from the curse of the fall through the atoning work of Jesus Christ at Calvary, the gospel of Jesus Christ likewise transforms our understanding and practice of leadership.

Jesus calls His followers to lead. Jesus taught that His followers were to be "the salt of the earth" and the "light of the world" (Matthew 5:13-14). Just as salt and light are penetrating agents, followers of Jesus are to be transforming agents on earth. When viewed through this lens, leadership can be defined as the movement of people to achieve the collective and mutual goals of transformation. Consequently, when we come to see leadership in this way, we can then accept that God calls, ordains, and uses us to lead others toward these purposes. At some level, and in different ways, each of us participates in the movement of individuals and groups of people toward some God-

ordained purpose. Some of us possess the God-given desire and ability to order and structure our environments for the achievement of God-given goals. Others may lead one person at a time. In either case, the purpose of leadership is to provide vision and direction for transformation—whether collectively or individually. Leaders are called to transform people, mind-sets, and the social environments in which people live, work, and interact.

Leadership development is an investment in the people of God. What is needed to build a Church Full of Leaders is a commitment to invest in the people of the congregation. Spiritual growth and maturity of members are the outcomes of a healthy church, and leadership development is one means by which members mature and become empowered to serve. In the revised edition of their book, *Leaders: Strategies for Taking Charge*, Warren Bennis and Burt Nanus define the transforming leader as one who "commits people to action, who converts followers into leaders and who may convert leaders into agents of change."[1] By developing leadership skills, members are better equipped to be used by God to change situations, structures, systems, and social milieus. Yes, each pastor's goal must become that of transforming followers into leaders and developing leaders who become agents of change.

Leadership development must be systematic. A systematic leadership development process is needed to build a Church Full of Leaders. An annual church leadership conference is not enough to infuse the spiritual, organizational, and interpersonal values and skills that are needed to fully develop the congregation. The effective development of leaders must be intentional and consistent. Leadership development that inculcates members in the vision and values of the church must become a part of the Christian education and formation strategy of the church. In leadership training, members build skills that enable them to participate in ministry processes by discovering their spiritual gifts as well as exploring opportunities to employ these gifts in ministry service.

Leadership development must be congruent with our understanding of leadership. How we develop leaders must be consistent with how we conceive of leadership. If we conceive of leadership as empowering, then our methods for developing and forming leaders must likewise be empowering. The leadership training must provide space for small-

group discussion and personal reflecting; topics must include basic leadership skills such as developing a vision, working with teams, resolving conflict, improving communication, as well as topics that are germane to a church's given context. For example, at one church the training included anti-racism topics aimed at helping congregants lead in a broader social context riddled by racism; issues of gender equality were included in the core training at another church. Still in another church, we might infuse principles of multicultural ministry into the entire curriculum.

Leading must become an expectation of the members of the congregation. In other words, leadership becomes normative for members of the congregation and leadership practice is infused throughout the church. In a Church Full of Leaders, congregants are helped to see every ministry of the church as transformative and to recognize the leadership dimension of each ministry. As a result, evangelism becomes leading people to Christ, not just inviting people to church. Worship becomes leading people into the presence of God. Discipleship becomes leading people to grow in their relationship with Christ. Teaching becomes leading people to truth and spiritual insight.

As one pastor said to members of his congregation at the inception of his church's leadership training process, "If you are not leading here in this church, you should be leading somewhere." So the expectation is given that on the job, in the community, or in the political arena, the believer is called to lead from the spiritual and ethical base provided by the church.

Building a Church Full of Leaders does not eliminate leadership positions such as pastor, director of children's ministry, or small-group ministry leader. These positions and similar positions are necessary in a Church Full of Leaders, as they help define the organizational and leadership structure and roles for a given church. In fact, the Church Full of Leaders series helps churches more effectively identify, select, train, and place people into formal ministry leadership positions in order to deliver more effective and transformative ministry. What is important, though, is that the people who fill these positions understand that leadership is more than a position. Leadership in a Church Full of Leaders is a process of visioning, structuring, organizing, and mobilizing men and women of God to accomplish the transformative purposes of God.

When we view leadership as a process, we come to see that it must be shared by more members in a ministry in order to optimize that ministry. Developing a Church Full of Leaders helps each congregant shift from seeing herself or himself as merely a member. Thus, this new understanding of their

roles as spiritual leaders helps increase their commitment to the success of the church's mission. *Building a Church Full of Leaders* helps all members begin to understand the structuring of the church, recognize their own "giftings" and "growing edges," and identify places within the ministry structure to which they may be called to serve. *Building a Church Full of Leaders* helps to equip more people for ministry—whether it's in the church, in the community, or in the marketplace.

People today need the church to support, equip, and sustain them as they work for transformation in their personal lives and their surrounding communities. The truly transforming church of the twenty-first century will need to build a Church Full of Leaders, in which each of us sees ourselves with leadership potential and is prepared to live out that potential in the various arenas of our lives. *Now imagine that!*

Chapter 2—Reflection

1. In what ways does the notion of a Church Full of Leaders challenge your traditional thinking about leadership?

2. In what ways have you been prepared and waiting for such a concept?

3. What opportunities for growth does this concept present for your church?

4. What resistance might your church express in response to such a concept?

5. Take some time to reflect on and pray about your responses to questions 1-4. Then in the space below, write out key things to keep in mind and watch for as you proceed with developing a Church Full of Leaders.

In order to build a Church Full of Leaders, you will need to develop a biblical yet practical perspective for developing leaders throughout your congregation.

Many religious and church leaders actually lead from their own implicit theories of leadership—notions about leadership they picked up from observing other leaders, perhaps their own pastors or their former bosses, or from reading a hodgepodge of articles and stories about leadership. Sometimes these implicit theories are derived from their personal interpretation of Scripture. For instance, while insisting that they base their leadership approach purely on Scripture, some pastors are unable to extract systematic and sustaining leadership principles from the pages of the sacred writ. Ironically, even their notions about biblical leadership may actually depend on their devotional reading for the week or their most current sermon series. One week, the pastor may justify his or her confrontational leadership style by citing how Jesus evicted the money changers from the temple. However, a few months later, that same pastor may teach conflict-entrenched church leaders to model Barnabas' encouraging style.

More typically, these implicit theories are based on tradition. For instance, many church leaders believe leadership is limited to a small group of people with special skills. Traditionally, these are the people who have always been in power in their own church context. For some pastors, this cadre of leaders may be limited to men over a certain age, to people with college degrees, or to outspoken women. Of course, these pastors would not admit that they hold these limiting beliefs. Many may not even be aware that they are the basis for their actions. In most cases, these unstated theories have not been examined, and the resulting concepts of leadership are ineffective for today's environment. But because "we have always done it this way," many pastors don't question or attempt to change their leadership patterns—unless they are forced to change. Rapid church growth, pastoral transitions, expanding ministries or dwindling membership, disengaged members, and unproductive ministry leaders cause pastors to examine their leadership and search for new ways of leading and developing leaders.

Toward a Theology of Leadership for a Church Full of Leaders

What is needed is a theological perspective of leadership and leadership development. The approach to church leadership for today's pastors must be explicit—the assumptions and claims must be stated so that pastors can examine and make informed choices about using the theory to guide his or her process of leadership development. The approach to church leadership for today's pastors must be biblically systematic—it must uncover patterns of leadership from

Scripture and in the experience of the church that provides guidance for the church. Finally, the approach to church leadership for today's church leaders must be practical—it must serve as a firm foundation upon which leadership development and training of church leaders can be based. The theological perspective upon which the *Building a Church Full of Leaders* series is based is explicit, systematic, and practical.

Leadership that is transformative is at the heart of biblical theology. Transformative leadership is a solid biblical and theological truth that has been overlooked when isolated biblical leaders or incidents are studied. When we look at the totality of God's story with God's people, what unfolds before us are marvelous truths about transformation and the people that God has enlisted in the transformative processes of creation, redemption, salvation (healing), and sanctification (maturing).

Biblical Examples of Transformative Leadership

Let's take a sampling of key epochs of biblical history: the Exodus, the Monarchy, the Post-exilic period, the first-century time of Jesus, and the time of the apostle Paul. Such leadership theology will have continuity with the past, yet be enacted in novel ways to address emerging exigencies for the church in each new era.

From the Exodus through the New Testament church age, each of these periods marked significant experiences in the life of the people of God. Each era called forth leaders who participated in God's work of changing people and circumstances to bring about God's purposes. During each period, the people of God needed to move from an old, oppressive, or outmoded state of being. They were given a vision of God's preferred future—a place of promise, of unity, and of new identity. In order to get to this new place, they were led into a place and process of preparation, training, and proving.

God called Moses and Joshua to lead the children of Israel out of Egypt, through the wilderness, and into the Promised Land. God used Deborah to liberate an oppressed community during the time of the judges. God used David to lead the formation of a united nation from a motley assortment of local tribes and communities. When Israel was exiled in Babylon, God used prophets such as Jeremiah and Isaiah to foretell of the new thing He was going to do to lead a second exodus through the wilderness and return His people to Jerusalem. God used Nehemiah to rally, organize, and direct people of the broken community to build up the walls of the city in order to unify the community. God not only sent Jesus as our atoning sacrifice, but also as the visionary who challenged the religious traditions of the status quo and cast a vision of God's kingdom on earth and in heaven. Jesus taught and trained a core group of men and women who would carry the vision for the church after His earthly departure. Finally, the apostle Paul not only played a key role in establishing churches, but he also gave us insight into the transforming work of the Holy Spirit in the life of the believer

as putting off our old selves, being transformed in our minds and attitudes, and putting on the new selves. In so doing, we move to a place of power and growth.

In each of these biblical examples, God transformed an old situation into a new one and used leaders who embraced transformation to help lead the change. Throughout biblical history, there were many other women and men who played a role in leading God's people, yet these six provide particularly helpful insights. The chart in Figure 2 summarizes the leadership challenges of these key biblical leaders. Notice in each of the situations above that God called or brought people out of the old and sent them through a transition in

Figure 2: Biblical Models of Transformative Leadership

Leader	Situation in Need of Change (Old Reality)	Transition	God's Preferred Future (New Reality)	Scripture Reference
Moses	Egyptian slavery	The wilderness experience and God's covenant	The Promised Land: people who were no longer slaves but now conquerors	Exodus
Deborah	Oppressed community	Organizing: defeating the enemy	Liberated community: a people whose perspective was opened up to God's possibilities	Judges 4 & 5
David	Scattered tribes/ nations	Organizing: nation building	A unified kingdom: an identity as victorious people of God	Samuel and Kings
Nehemiah	Broken community	Building the city: working together	A re-established community	Nehemiah
Jesus	Religious tradition invested in the status quo	Training, testing, and empowerment at Pentecost	The kingdom of God as lived out by the church: a people of faith who extended the work of Christ through the Holy Spirit	The Gospels, Acts
Paul	Old selves	Renewal of the mind and attitudes that comes from new relationship in Christ with each other	New selves: a maturing people of God called to be the church, with a new mind-set reflected in a new lifestyle	Ephesians 4:19-23

order to bring them into the new. Though simplified for our purposes, this three-part process helps us to understand the core elements of the process of transformation, and thus the requirements of transformative leadership: 1) a vision of a new reality; 2) an understanding of the current state; and 3) a strategy for movement of people toward that vision.

This same three-part process of transformation can be instructive for today's church leaders who desire to implement change in their churches. Every church leader must understand the current situation in which he or she is leading and understand clearly what is not working in it. Every church leader must spend time in prayer to get a vision of what God is intending to do to address the contradictions of the current situation. Then, finally, church leaders today must lead their people through a process of transformative steps and stages, as did the leaders of old.

Taking a closer look at these examples of biblical transformation, we see that in each case, the leader who was charged with providing direction did not accomplish the work on his or her own but enlisted other leaders into the process. Moses had Joshua and Caleb (Numbers 13), as well as the leaders of thousands, hundreds, fifties, and tens (Exodus 18:14-26). Deborah had Barak (Judges 4&5). David had his mighty men of valor (1 Samuel 23:13; 2 Samuel 10:6) that started out as a group of 400 distressed, debt-ridden malcontents (1 Samuel 22:1). Nehemiah had leaders of squads of workers stationed strategically around the wall of Jerusalem (Nehemiah 3). Jesus had His disciples and the twelve apostles (Matthew 10:1-2; Luke 6:11-16; Acts 1:2; 2:37). Paul had Timothy, Titus, Aquila, Priscilla (Acts 18:18; Romans 16:3), Phoebe (Romans 16:1) and other fellow laborers (Romans 16:6-16) who helped to build the churches of God. These leaders show us that the more significant the work of transformation, the more critical the need to enlist other leaders in the process. So too must today's leaders engage other transformative leaders in the process for the effects of change to ripple throughout the congregation. The more significant the work of transformation, the more critical will be the need to enlist other leaders in the process.

The diagram in Figure 3 is a model of transformation that serves as a visual tool for grasping the key points of transformation summarized in the previous chart.

Transformation: Bringing Forth the New

As we have seen, biblical notions of transformation always involve movement from one place to another. Yet it is more than just physical movement; it is existential and spiritual movement that makes an impact on people's understanding of their new identity, their purpose for being, and their authority and ability to thrive in this new place. It is an ontological movement.

Today's church leaders must work toward transformation in order to accomplish the purposes of God. If Moses (and Joshua) had just facilitated the physical movement of the Hebrews out of Egypt and into the Promised Land, they would have participated in the transportation of millions of people. However, transportation of the body without the accompanying "transportation" of attitudes and mind-sets is not transformation. Instead, it was God's intent to transform these people from slaves into conquerors. This type of transformation is an internal change of heart and mind, attitudes and thoughts that ultimately affect an outer change of behavior.

Sadly, many of today's leaders are merely transporting God's people from program to program, activity to activity, even from church building to larger church building with no ensuing or accompanying transformation. An individual leader cannot accomplish this great transformation alone. *Building a Church Full of Leaders* requires the transformation of the pastor and every leader of the congregation.

What is needed is a means of moving people out of their old ways and into a way of being and ministering that simultaneously fulfills the church's mandate and the individual's purpose. Too often, pastors have attempted to fulfill the church's mandate at the expense of the people's purpose. The people were seen to be disposable and dispensable. No longer can we afford to squander, abuse, and misuse the precious gifts that are in our congregations. It is time to invest in the people in the pews in order to gain a future return for the sake of a more effective shared ministry. Transformative leadership is mutually empowering,

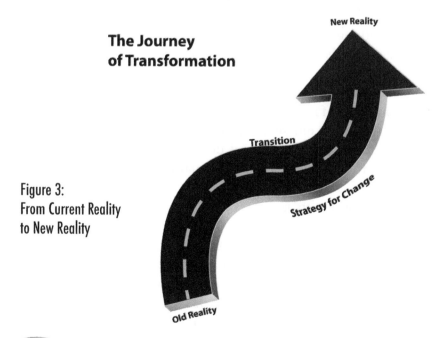

The Journey of Transformation

New Reality

Transition

Strategy for Change

Old Reality

Figure 3:
From Current Reality
to New Reality

and it leads the congregation toward a clearer purpose, power, and maturity—both individually and collectively.

As mentioned in the previous chapter, Warren Bennis and Burt Nanus, authors of *Leaders: Strategies for Taking Charge,* give us insight into this process, defining what transformative leadership looks like. Again, pastors need ways to commit members of the congregation to active service, and *Building a Church Full of Leaders* uses the theories and practices of transformative leadership to help pastors develop leaders who become change agents for the cause of Christ. As we see it, the transformative leader helps to move people from passively sitting in the pews to actively serving and leading, and in so doing the people move in their understanding of who they are and why they have been called to the church.

The type of change required to build a Church Full of Leaders starts internally and manifests outwardly, for that is at the root of biblical notions of transformation. *Morphe,* the Greek root word from which we translate our English word "transformation," emphasizes an inward change. Jim Herrington, R. Robert Creech, and Trisha Taylor, authors of *The Leader's Journey: Accepting the Call to Personal and Congregational Transformation,* define transformation as a "change in an individual, a church or community that alters both the mental model one uses to view the world and one's behavior in the world."[1] Indeed, transformative leadership requires a change of the heart, mind, attitude, and perspective. It requires a letting go of models and habits that no longer work and embracing a new way of seeing and doing that emanates from a new way of seeing and being in the world. It is leading from the inside out.

The Lord declares to us, "Look, I am making all things new!" (Revelation 21:5). The Lord declared through the prophet Isaiah to the nation in exile, "For I am about to do something new.
See, I have already begun!" (Isaiah 43:19). The apostle Paul affirmed that anyone in Christ is a new creation—"old things are passed away; behold, all things are become new" (2 Corinthians 5:17, KJV). The resurrection of Christ reaffirms and reinforces the promises of newness, yet for some reason we get stuck in old ways and old habits that block our success. Instead of trying to dress up dead, tired programs, transformative leaders must develop processes that call forth new ideas and energy from people who are continually being made new.

Key Assumptions of Transformative Leadership

God's Sovereignty. The sovereign God leads the work of transformation and enlists us into the process. God chooses the person that He will use based on His work of grace—not our gender, race, ethnicity, social class, or personality. This key assumption helps the leader accept that the work of the church is God's work, and God has enlisted us in a

process that is led by Him. This insight helps to free the leader to trust and follow the leading of the Lord.

God's Revelation. God reveals a preferred or future reality that is better than what we currently have. God's preferred reality provides ministry leaders with a vision for ministry. The pastor will not be the only one to see what God wants to do on behalf of hurting people. However, the pastor must lead the process by which the various glimpses of the vision are integrated to create a fuller picture.

God's Calling of a Royal Priesthood. God calls all believers into ministry, thus inviting all of the people of God to join in leading in various dimensions of the church. Each of us has a different role. All may not have the title of "leader," but each of us must work together to accomplish the purposes of leadership. God prepares and qualifies us for leadership through our own process of transformation that entails building and working through relationships as we serve in and for the church. In the process, God uses wilderness time, training time, separations, and reconciliations to transform us for His work.

God's Story. Transformation is at the heart of the story of God's relationship with humankind. God has always called and used leaders to participate in the transformation of humans and society. *Building a Church Full of Leaders* must be established upon a foundation that will sustain the movement of the people of God toward the vision of God. In order to do this, more members of the congregation must be transformed and equipped to fulfill their calling to lead.

A systematic theology of leadership must inform the practice of leadership. Take some time, as you prepare to identify and develop leaders in the congregation, to review the leadership lessons from Scripture as well as from the history of the church. Name and examine your assumptions about leadership—make the implicit explicit. The clearer you are on what constitutes church leadership or even Christian leadership, the more clearly you can convey those principles to develop a Church Full of Leaders in line with the God-given vision for your church.

Chapter 3—Reflection

1. Think of a picture, image, or symbol that comes to mind when you think about a leader. In the space below, draw this picture. Then list key qualities or characteristics that support this image.

2. Reflect on your image of a leader and the qualities you expect in a leader. Then complete the following statements:

    Leaders are

    Leaders must

    Leaders should

    Your responses to questions 1 and 2 may be useful in helping to uncover your implicit theory about leadership. Keep them in mind as you complete other segments of the handbook. As you continue, it will be useful to evaluate how valid these ideas about leadership are for your current leadership context.

3. Reflect on leadership images or stories from Scripture that guide your thinking about church leadership. How do these key images inform your practice of leadership and your expectations for leaders?

4. Pastoral transition, rapid church growth, dwindling church membership, disengaged members, and unproductive leaders call forth the need for

change. Which of these needs for change describe your reasons for wanting to develop a Church Full of Leaders? What are some other reasons you need to change the way you approach and develop leaders?

5. Based on what you have just read, develop a definition of transformative leadership using your own words and experiences. Think of a few examples to illustrate this concept for your people.

6. Re-read the section "Key Assumptions of Transformative Leadership." Which of these assumptions do you really believe and buy into? Take a few moments to express why. Which of these assumptions do you have difficulty buying into? Take a few moments to express your difficulty.

Strategic Organizing

one

M inistries must be strategic. To be strategic, they must be organized to fulfill their mission. Leaders of strategic ministries tap into the heart and mind of God to discern the direction God is taking the church and to receive from God the strategy for moving the church in that direction.

A strategy is a plan for realizing a vision or achieving a goal. In any given realm or endeavor, a strategy in that arena takes into account the interconnected systems and layers (strata) that affect that arena. For instance, to keep peace in a given region of the world, the United Nations will develop a strategy that employs the political, economic, psychological, and military forces of a nation or group of nations to ensure support and advancement of the policies it deems necessary to maintain peace in that region. So too must the church take into account and address the spiritual matrix that blocks people from the light and truth of God, the various systems and strata of society that affect the people the church is called to draw.

Strategic ministry is accomplished through people. No longer, even in small to medium-sized churches, and especially in growing small or start-up churches, can pastors accomplish effective ministry alone. To be effective, there must be a structure and systematic process for organizing the people through whom and with whom ministry will be accomplished. Structure and process is to the church what the skeletal and circulatory systems are to the human body—they hold the body together and ensure proper internal movement of vital life forces.

Engaging people in ministry is a spiritual issue, but it also must be strategic, systematic, and structured. Service in the church isn't mere volunteerism—it's a call. Drawing believers to serve isn't just recruitment—it's discipleship. Doing our part to carry out the mission of our local church, particularly as leaders, is not simply about doing church work. It is about effectively spreading the gospel and helping believers to mature spiritually and fulfill their purpose as servants of God. So strategically organizing an effective ministry that enlists and places our church members into service is important.

In this section of the Church Full of Leaders handbook, we will introduce you to a strategic organizing model, provide you with a biblical model for organizing the ministry processes of your church, give you a means of gaining insight into the context and people to whom your church ministers, and delineate key ministry processes, such as ministry engagement and other administrative processes.

Church leadership strategy flows from the theological perspective of the church and its leadership. In churches that are framed around the centrality of pastoral leadership, pastors are called as overseers of the church or congregation. It is their calling and purpose to hear from God for the congregation.

God has placed pastors in the body and over specific churches to lead His people. As such, a pastor is an overseer, "one who sees over" or governs a church. Pastors are shepherds who serve under the Chief Shepherd and watch over the souls of the flock (1 Peter 5:4; Hebrew 13:17). The pastor governs or leads the congregation, having been given authority by God (Hebrews 13:7, 17). Any leadership that is exercised within a church does so under the auspices and sanctioning of pastoral leadership. Individual leaders within a church are accountable to and responsible to the pastor.

How pastoral leaders organize themselves and their churches may stem from denominational traditions or issues related to size and complexity. For instance, some churches organize ministry such that pastors are ministers of word and sacrament and their key charge is to perform or oversee the performance of preaching, sacraments, and pastoral care, while ruling elders oversee, lead and perform operational and administrative duties with the congregation.

Other churches are structured around a pastoral model that blends shepherding and executive functions of ministry and clergy and lay staff are organized around these areas of ministry.

Priesthood of All Believers

But you are a chosen generation, a royal priesthood, a holy nation, His own special people, that you may proclaim the praises of Him who called you out of darkness into His marvelous light. (1 Peter 2:9, NKJV)

Churches anchored in the theological premise of the priesthood of all believers aim to engage all members at some level of ministry, believing that every member is gifted and called to serve. The strategy for these churches is to engage members into ministry, giving them avenues for exercising their gifts and talents. These churches will often use a very decentralized model of ministry in which ministry teams are led by lay members and key decisions are left in the hands of congregational members active on these ministry teams. This approach to ministry is often common in small to medium-sized churches.

Organizing Strategy: Professional Staff and Lay Leadership

Healthy churches grow, and with growth there comes the need to add staff and begin to centralize ministry leadership and decisions. This is a model in which the pastoral staff consists of ministers and professionals that handle the administrative, operational, and developmental activities of the church. In these churches ministry programs and processes, especially educational and connective ministries, are led by lay leaders and members gifted in these areas. They receive support from paid staff who develop leaders, provide assistance with program development, and handle administrative and operational issues.

Organizing Strategy: Regionalization vs Geographic Centers

To either facilitate or stir growth, church leaders need to be intentional about their organizing strategy. Some churches use a strategy in which the church becomes a regional center and attracts members from a broad region. The church becomes the central destination for the faith community's spiritual development.

Other churches use a strategy of building multiple sites throughout the region. Each site becomes the spiritual center for a segment of the congregation. In this way, the brand of the church remains but a church may minister to believers in a suburb and those in a city at the same time

Organizing Strategy: Online Presence and Virtual Membership

In today's highly mobile society, people connect via Internet and social media to institutions in ways that were unheard of in previous generations. Technology allows us to connect with a host of believers: upwardly mobile professionals required to relocate frequently, college students who go away for several years, people across the globe. Regardless of size, more and more church leaders must think about integrating online technology into their outreach, discipleship, connectional, and service strategies. The Church Full of Leaders approach to leadership development fits well into these strategic approaches to ministry and leadership.

Implicit within a strategy is an approach or perspective about the issues the strategy is aimed at addressing. Strategy entails methodology—or a broad-based approach for comprehensively solving a problem or reaching a goal. Ministry is the church's methodology for saving souls; delivering, healing, and renewing minds; and empowering people. Today's church leaders must minister smarter (through the wisdom of God) than the enemy of our souls. The ministry strategy, then, is the prayer-soaked, comprehensive plan that articulates the church's God-given vision, mission, core values, and approaches for moving people through the spiritual and social barriers, or opposition, toward God's vision God's way.

The graphic in Figure 4 helps us to understand a strategic model for organizing a transformative church. Just as a hub is core to a wheel, at the core of the church's strategy is a clear articulation of mission, vision, and core values. Together these define who the church is, what it has been called to do,

Figure 4

CFOL Strategic Organizing Wheel

Leadership & Direction Setting Processes

Ministry Structure & Organizing Systems

Mission
Vision
Core Values

Transformative Ministry Processes

People Equipping Processes

and what it aims to accomplish. And just as spokes emanate from the hub, there are four main spokes that reinforce the church's leadership strategy:

Spoke 1: Leadership and Direction Setting Processes—the vision casting and direction setting function of the church.

Spoke 2: Transformative Ministry Processes—the heart of ministry, the means by which people are transformed by and for service.

Spoke 3: Ministry Structure and Organizing Systems—the ministry infrastructure is the skeletal system of the body of Christ. These are the systems and structures used to organize the transformative ministries of the church.

Spoke 4: People Equipping Processes—the preparation, training, and development arm of the church.

Now, let's look at each segment in detail.

The Strategy Hub

Mission, Vision, Core Values. At the core of every ministry or church is an approach to ministry that gets communicated in your statements about mission, vision, core values, as well as in your strategic ministry plans and goals.

- The church mission statement is critical to articulating and sharing the focus and purpose of your church.

- The vision statement helps you share the direction of your church with key stakeholders, including members, visitors, and community members.

- Core values articulate the fundamental beliefs and principles of the church.

Understanding the Mission for Your Church

Jesus came to proclaim the gospel of the kingdom of God to the entire world. He fulfilled His mission and has passed His mission onto His church. Just as the church of Jesus Christ has a mission and purpose, so does every local church. Your church has been called into existence for a specific, distinct, and unique purpose. As the pastor, you have been charged with reaching people with the gospel of Jesus Christ and participating with the work of the Holy Spirit to transform the lives of people and communities. Let's see what the Bible has to say about the mission of the church of Jesus Christ.

Called Out to Carry Forth the Mission of Jesus

The church is an assembly of followers of Jesus Christ called out to carry forth the mission of Jesus. Matthew 4:24 describes the mission of our Lord: "he went about all Galilee, teaching in their synagogues, preaching the gospel of the kingdom, and healing all kinds of sickness and all kinds of diseases." According to Matthew, the mission of Jesus was to teach, preach, and heal.

Jesus gives insight into His mission: "The Spirit of the Lord is upon Me, because He has anointed Me to preach the gospel to the poor; He has sent Me to heal the brokenhearted, to proclaim liberty to the captives and recovery of sight to the blind, to set at liberty those who are oppressed; to proclaim the acceptable year of the Lord" (Luke 4:18-19, NKJV). Jesus came to earth to preach, heal, and proclaim liberty and recovery.

The heart of the gospel message is that Jesus came to earth to die for the sins of the world and save all who would believe on Him from sin and the holding power of Satan. The good news that Jesus brought is also known as the

gospel of the kingdom, because this good news of salvation is ultimately about the governing power of God in the lives of those who surrender to the Lord. The good news of the kingdom (or reign, rule, and governing power of God) is that bad news people can now embrace good news, wayward people can be taught the life-changing principles of God, the hearts of broken people can be mended, the sick can be healed, the oppressed can be liberated—the coming and continued presence of Jesus makes it all a reality for each of us who believes!

Jesus proclaimed that He would establish His church, against which the gates of hell would never prevail (Matthew 16:18). The mission of the church of Jesus Christ is to advance the victorious message in spite of the assaults of the powers of darkness. Jesus already has assured us of victory against the power of death and hell, because He conquered death, hell, and the grave (Ephesians 4: 7-10; 1 Corinthians 15:57).

The writer to the Ephesians gives us an additional insight into the mission of the church: "According to the eternal purpose which He accomplished in Christ Jesus our Lord," God intends for the church to make known the manifold wisdom of God" (Ephesians 3:11, NKJV). The church is to be the instrument for dispensing God's wisdom before the world and all evil powers. Every local church then must stay so connected to the plan, power, and provision of God through prayer and worship, that the church truly dispenses God's mind and message for the age.

In fact, Jesus commissioned His disciples (i.e., Jesus sent them forth with a mission) by commanding them to "[g]o and make disciples of all the nations" (Matthew 28:19-20, NKJV). The disciples, or followers, of Jesus the world over constitute the church. We are the collection of followers committed to carry forth the mission of Jesus, and we are called to teach the commandments of Christ with the promise that He will always be with us.

Finally, the writer to the Ephesians teaches us about the leadership gifts Christ gave to the church—apostles, prophets, evangelists, pastors, and teachers. These leaders are charged with equipping the saints for the work of ministry. In other words, these leaders are to prepare and help make the saints or followers of Christ fit for the ministry of the church, and together through ministry the saints edify or build up the body of Christ or the church. In this sense the church is a dynamic, living organism sustained by its members who are connected to and through the Holy Spirit. One further function of the church is to edify its members and itself, creating a symbiotic relationship and connection between itself and its members. Later in Chapter 5, we will examine the ministries of the church and the role they play in edifying or building up the body of Christ. Perhaps the following graphic in Figure 5 will help to pull it all together for you:

So What's Your Mission?

Some people argue that every church has but one mission, and that is the mission of the church of Jesus Christ—to proclaim the good news of the kingdom of God as revealed in Jesus Christ by making known the manifold wisdom of God, extending the anointed teaching, preaching, and healing ministry of Jesus and withstanding the evil forces of hell. Yet we know that each local congregation fulfills this mandate in ways that are particular to its cultural and social context. In fact, each local church is called to extend the mission of Jesus in a specific community or region. The ways in which you have been called to fulfill the mission of Jesus in a specific cultural and social context is what the mission statement captures. At some level, your mission statement must reflect the universal mission of the church, yet at the same time your mission statement must convey the particular cultural and social contexts in which you serve.

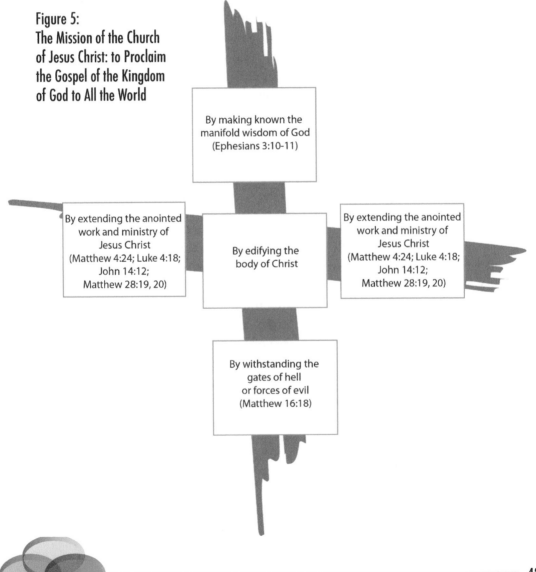

Figure 5:
The Mission of the Church of Jesus Christ: to Proclaim the Gospel of the Kingdom of God to All the World

By making known the manifold wisdom of God (Ephesians 3:10-11)

By extending the anointed work and ministry of Jesus Christ (Matthew 4:24; Luke 4:18; John 14:12; Matthew 28:19, 20)

By edifying the body of Christ

By extending the anointed work and ministry of Jesus Christ (Matthew 4:24; Luke 4:18; John 14:12; Matthew 28:19, 20)

By withstanding the gates of hell or forces of evil (Matthew 16:18)

Defining the Mission of Your Church

A mission statement, then, articulates the focus of a specific church. A well-defined mission statement helps leaders and members understand:

- **the church's character**—who you are and who you are not
- **the church's causes**—what you stand for and don't stand for
- **the church's commitments**—what you do and what you don't do
- **the church's capabilities**—the needs that your church meets through its ministries

Mission statements are developed in a variety of ways, depending upon the leadership style that predominates in the church. For some churches, the governing board develops and revises the mission statement. For other churches, the pastor develops the mission statement with review by other members of the pastoral staff. Whatever your process for developing such a statement, it will be helpful to review and/or refine your mission statement prior to embarking upon a comprehensive leadership development process. The more leaders you involve in the process, the more clarity and ownership you eventually get around the mission. The questions at the end of this chapter will help you develop or refine your mission statement using a facilitated group process.

After you have developed or refined your mission, you must prayerfully identify a systematic way of sharing, teaching, and clarifying this mission with the members, and current and potential leaders of your church. Following are a few suggestions for bringing the mission to life for your congregation:

1. Embark upon a congregational Bible study or teaching series on the mission of the church and share your church's current, new, or refined mission statement. Don't forget to show how your mission statement fulfills the key dimensions of Christ's mission.
2. Make the church's mission a focus theme for a month. Hold special teaching sessions for leaders and teachers, and charge each ministry leader and teacher to teach, share, and discuss the mission in their upcoming monthly meetings.
3. Display the mission in a prominent place in the church; place the mission statement in an appropriate place on the church bulletin board, Web site, and other internal and external communication vehicles of the church.
4. Design a bookmark with the church's mission statement and provide the bookmark as a takeaway for each member and visitor during the church mission emphasis month.

Writing the Mission Statement

Your ears shall hear a word behind you, saying, "This is the way, walk in it," ~Isaiah 30:21, NKJV

Forgetting your mission leads, inevitably, to getting tangled up in details—details that can take you completely off your path. ~Laurie Beth Jones, The Path

Six Elements of a Good Mission Statement:

Need-directed—every mission implies that someone is helped and the mission statement must reflect the fulfillment of a need for some group or population of people.

Value-based—every mission must be fueled by passion and the mission statement must reflect the core values of your organization.

Active—every mission requires action and the mission statement should reflect the primary actions or service activities of the ministry.

Succinct—a good mission statement articulates your ministry's primary purpose and should be no more than a single sentence long.

Understandable—a good mission statement should be easily understood by a twelve-year-old.

Memorable—a good mission statement should be able to be recited by memory at a moment's notice.

Suggested Mission Statement Template

The mission of the _____ is to:

_____

(action words that reflect the ministry)

_____

(core value(s) of the ministry)

To, for, or with

_____

(the group or population to whom you are called)

Sample Mission Statements

The mission of Greater Faith Church is to provide a church home where relationships are nurtured in a warm family atmosphere; to demonstrate through the preaching and teaching of the Word of God that people can be changed emotionally, spiritually, and physically; to create an atmosphere of worship that increases greater faith in God and cultivates spiritual growth; and to show that, through Christ, everyone in our church is loved and needed to fulfill the Great Commission.

The mission of New Life Church is to bring unbelievers into the full knowledge and acceptance of Jesus Christ and to create disciples who are equipped to transform the community into a New Life by establishing a worshiping, Bible-believing, multicultural, holistic ministry that nurtures individuals to spiritual maturity, serves the community, restores households, and ignites families into divine purpose.

Articulating a Vision for Ministry

Vision is the perspective the leader possesses as she or he comes to see what God has ordained and planned for his or her work. Vision is seeing what God shows you.

When leaders are said to be people of vision, we are referring to their ability to paint a picture of a future possibility for the church. If a pastor is to build a Church Full of Leaders, the pastor must envision a future for the church that is different, greater, and more powerful than its present state. Vision is an in-depth understanding of where the church is going—a realistic, credible, attractive future for your church that focuses on transformation. A vision statement is your articulation of a destination toward which you see God moving your church.

This future state of the church is a powerful, galvanizing force to move the church forward and motivate members by calling them to action and greater commitment. Once the vision is set, you must secure a vision or picture of the type of leadership that will be necessary in your envisioned church.

A vision for transformative ministry to the people you have been assigned starts with prayer. This type of life-changing ministry can only be conceived through heart-stirring communication with the Master Transformer. It is only through spending intense time in the presence of God, that the leader taps into the plans of God and hears and feels the heart of God for people. Only when the leader's mind, imagination, and heart have been saturated with God's love and purposes will the leader be able to envision the transformative ministry that God has for people.

The leader must also spend time with the people, to allow God to show him or her the heart needs of the people—not the needs the people project or

display. As a leader spends time with the people to whom he or she has been assigned, the leader cultivates a desire and discipline to hear the people's hearts and takes those heart musings to God.

Through prayer, God will reveal God's plan for ministering to the people and will give the leader a vision for carrying forth that plan. The leader must be in tune with the Holy Spirit as the Spirit plants a thought or idea into the mind and heart of the leader. Every God-ordained and sanctioned ministry started with a thought from God!

When the vision comes from God in the form of a thought or idea for ministry or an overwhelming desire or burden for change, the wise leader will write down these thoughts, or ideas, and continue seeking God to unfold the full vision. Remember, God told Habakkuk to "write the vision and make it plain." Some people get a glimpse and try to run with it, only to find that neither they nor the people running with them were clear on the vision. Running with fuzzy vision can prove disastrous. Committing thoughts to paper helps to capture the idea and is the first crucial step to bringing the vision to life. Just as the thought manifests in written symbols upon paper, so will the vision manifest into reality for the faithful leader who follows God's plan.

The next step for bringing about a vision for ministry is preparation. God told Habakkuk to make it plain, so that they that run could read it. This step entails forming the teams, identifying the necessary resource, and developing the plans for carrying out the envisioned ministry. Much of the remaining portions of this manual are devoted to developing the leadership skills for planning and carrying out ministry. Just remember, transformative ministry starts with a vision for transformation that flows directly from the heart of God!

Creating the Vision Statement

> *Where there is no vision, the people perish. ~Proverbs 29:18*
> *Write the vision and make it plain. ~Habakkuk 2:2*

Visionary leaders start with the end in mind. Visionary leaders take time to listen to God to understand where God wants to take the people of the church or ministry.

A Vision Statement...

- Provides focus for the church, leaders, and ministries
- Helps leaders communicate the ministry themes to a broader audience
- Communicates thematic emphasis for program leaders

Sample Vision Statements

The Greater Faith Church Vision Statement

The Greater Faith Church is a worshipping church of the Pentecostal tradition serving the greater tri-state region. We are committed to building a place of healing for broken people needing emotional and spiritual support. We seek to unify communities, businesses and God-fearing believers to work together for the betterment of the lives of people in our community.

New Life Church Vision Statement

It is our aim and desire to establish a safe haven to which people come to be transformed and renewed in their mind, to be healed emotionally, spiritually, and psychologically. It is our vision that members of New Life will become servant ministers, active in serving Christ by serving the church and by sharing the gospel through witnessing. It is our vision that members of New Life will be fruitful and lead prosperous lives.

Core Values

At the heart of every ministry are values that represent the guiding principles for the local church or ministry. These guiding principles are foundational to a given church and help convey the distinctive character of that church. Core values are the elements or principles of a church that are non-negotiable. These values may reflect theological and doctrinal statements of a church, beliefs about the ways people should be served, and the expectations for leaders and members of the congregation. Core values convey to members the set of principles that link them together, as well as communicate to visitors and newcomers a set of expectations for entering into and participating in that church.

Sample Core Values Statements

- **Greater Faith Church Core Values**

  The Church. The church of Jesus Christ is God's vehicle for bringing a lost world back to God. We commit to building a community of love within the church, and spreading the love of that community out to the world.

  The Bible. The Bible is the inspired Word of God that provides insight and wisdom for every facet of our lives. We order our personal and communal lives by the principles of the Word of God.

Faith. Faith is crucial to the life of every believer and is the primary means by which we bring into reality the plans and purposes of God. We meditate and act upon the Word of God, thus being strengthened in our faith and empowered to do God's will.

Teaching. Anointed teaching is the primary catalyst for transformation in the lives of individuals and in the church. We thus put priority on teaching and helping members order their lives according to the principles of the Word of God.

Servant Leadership. God orders the affairs of the church of Jesus Christ through leaders. Therefore, it is our charge to prepare members for leadership in the church, in our communities and surrounding workplaces.

- **Core Values of New Life Church**

Truth. People are seeking truth and the New Life Church strives to "keep it real." Through honest, authentic ministry, New Life helps people to be real with themselves and with God.

Love. New Life demonstrates the love of Christ in welcoming its guests as well as one another. Hugs, smiles and other gestures are evidence of the love that is shared. The demonstration of love communicates to members and visitors that they are valued and cared for.

Worship. Worship is a priority at New Life—singing, preaching, praying. We believe the presence of God brings freedom and breakthrough. In our public worship, the services prepare us to receive the Word and lead us to continual repentance and change. The leaders strive to maintain the unity of the Spirit (Ephesians 4:3) and do not tolerate or encourage grandstanding. The focus is on God and everything we do points to God and to the Word.

Liberty. New Life has cultivated an environment of freedom in which people have the liberty to be themselves. This environment is free of judgment and is a place of safety for getting help and wholeness.

Accountability. New Life is accountable to its members in our church and leadership practices. Our accountability extends to and is not limited to operational, administrative, and financial decisions. We plan, we serve, and we lead with the good of the church in mind, being prepared to give an account to God and the people for our decisions.

Leadership and Direction-Setting Processes

Each church needs a leadership structure. It might consist of your board of trustees, the pastoral staff, board of elders, and/or the ministry leaders. These groups help to cast the vision and set the direction for the church or ministry. They are accountable for the ministry and for developing processes through which the work of ministry is accomplished.

These are the processes senior leaders use to organize leaders, and develop communication channels in order to share vision and direction to ministry leaders and the congregation. In a Church Full of Leaders, the aim is to invite more and more people into the leadership processes of the church. Consequently, clear structures and processes must be in place in order to keep leaders at every level aligned with the direction of senior leadership. Some of the major functions of the leadership and direction setting processes include:

- providing thought leadership around the aspirational elements of the church
- defining and developing the church's ministry strategy and setting goals
- ensuring competence of leaders at all levels
- positioning the church in the communities in which it serves

Transformative Ministry Processes

Prayer, evangelism, worship, discipleship, fellowship, and service are the core ministry processes of the church that transform people's lives. Every church needs these ministries, and must be organized to effectively deliver these ministries. Transformative ministry starts and ends with prayer. For purposes of organizing ministry functions, we will place prayer and worship ministries together, as they are vital dimensions of setting the spiritual tone of the church and providing the means by seeking and asking God's direction for the church. Some of the major functions of the transformative ministry processes include:

- optimizing the church's success with transforming the lives of people it serves
- strategically positioning the church to understand and penetrate emerging needs in the community
- enabling the church's ministries and membership to develop and deliver services that meet the needs of increasingly diverse communities

Ministry Structure and Organizing Systems

Every ministry must have administrative, operational, and support services in order to deliver ministry. These processes help to provide the infrastructure necessary for building a strong church. Basic organizing processes include administration, communication, financial development and tracking, media,

technology, and facilities management. As the ministry or church grows more complex, additional organizing processes may be developed to coordinate the various dimensions of the ministry. Some of the major functions of the ministry structure and organizing systems include:

- gathering and reporting information that informs ministry leaders of progress on goals
- communicating ministry initiatives, actions, and successes to church leadership and membership on a timely basis
- leveraging structures that optimize the church's success with transformative ministry, such as ministry ad staff training

For these functions organizing schemes are documented in organizational charts, and role and position descriptions. These structures are not meant to put people in boxes, but they are intended to provide clarity as to how ministry is performed, they provide clarity for communication, development, and operating.

The remaining chapters in this section are aimed at explaining the transformative ministry processes and developing structures for organizing these ministries.

People Equipping Processes

According to Ephesians 4:11-12, leaders are placed in the church in order to equip the saints for the work of ministry. Transformative ministries systematically and intentionally prepare people of the congregation to do the work of ministry. These ministries develop leaders and workers, continually develop the ministries of the church, and implement a systematic means of training and placing people into ministry service. They identify ministry and leadership competencies that are necessary to do the work of ministry to move the church toward its God-given vision. Some of the major functions of the people equipping processes include:

- facilitating the church's/ministry's goals of attracting, developing, and retaining competent spiritually mature leaders who serve at every level
- ensuring that men and women from a variety of ethnic, cultural, and social backgrounds can contribute to the church/ministry's success
- creating and sustaining a transforming culture/worship environment

How people are equipped for ministry is essential. Having a systematic approach to the development and training of members and leaders is essential. Church leaders need an intentional plan or strategy for equipping people to serve

and lead in each of the transformative ministry functions. Often the first part of equipping people to serve is helping them identify their own giftedness and getting them plugged into a complementary area of ministry. Other equipping functions include training leaders and leadership team members and orienting members to serving in specific ministries.

Sections two and three of this manual, covers the spiritual development processes leaders need to remain consistent in and the key skills necessary for effective collaborative ministry. Strategic organizing is a critical first step of strengthening your church. Leaders of your church must understand the mission, vision, and values as they guide them on how they operate and fulfill the tasks of ministry.

Chapter 4—Reflection

1. Consider forming a Church Full of Leaders Vision Team to help you write or refine your mission, vision, and core values. Who might be best to serve on this team?

2. Review the elements of a good mission statement on page 34. If you currently have a mission statement, is your current statement need-directed? Value-based? Active? Succinct? Memorable? If not, how might you modify the statement?

3. Do you have a church vision statement? Consider the following areas as you seek God about the direction for your church.

   Church Goals—1, 3 and 5 years out

   - Leadership
   - Ministries
   - People Equipping Processes & Staffing
   - Administration
   - Church Building and Grounds
   - Finances
   - Systems
   - Other

   Now write a statement that reflects the core or essence of the goals you have prayerfully established.

4. What are the core values or the "non-negotiables" of your church?

   - Doctrinal Points
   - Leadership Principles
   - Ministry Principles
   - Serving Principles
   - Others:

Areas to contemplate in developing your ministry strategy:

(1)   Leadership/Direction Setting Process

- Describe your current leadership structure. Is it adequate for the direction the church is taking? How might it need to change?
- Ministries will emerge to meet the needs of the people. How will you organize these ministries and train these emergent ministry leaders?

(2)   Ministry Structure and Organizing Systems

How are you currently structured? Is your current leadership structure individual-based or team-based? How might you transition to a team based leadership structure? As you continue to grow, you will need to add staff. What plan do you have in place for adding staff (paid and/or volunteer)? What resources do you need to develop a financial plan that funds new paid staff?

(3)   Transformative Ministry Processes

Are your ministries meeting the needs of the congregation and community? What new ministries are needed?

(4)   People Equipping Processes

Training of volunteer and paid staff is critical. What plan needs to be in place to continue investing in the people who lead in and serve your congregation and community?

The record of the church given to us in the New Testament provides us with insight into five foundational ministry functions of the church (Figure 6). At their core, these ministries are transformative—full engagement in them leads to changing people's lives. These five processes are the crux of ministry—the ways in which we serve God and the people of God. They have at their heart leadership dimensions that help to define their nature and fundamental purposes. It is these ministries that help to make the church the distinct entity it is. Taken together, these five ministry functions lead to edification, or building up of the church and the people of the church.

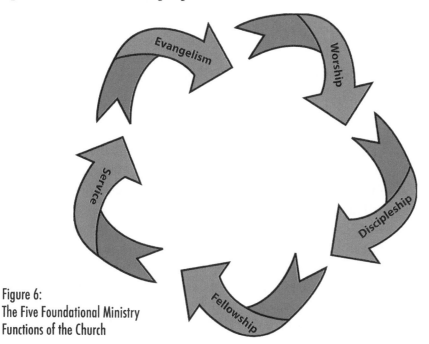

Figure 6:
The Five Foundational Ministry
Functions of the Church

These ministries are summarized in Figure 7. Let's look at each in more detail.

Evangelism

The followers of Jesus Christ were commanded to preach the gospel. The Greek word for gospel is *euangelion,* and its verb form, *euangelo,* is the active proclamation of the gospel, or good news of Jesus Christ. In his epistle to the Romans, the apostle Paul defined the gospel as "the power of God unto salvation" to all people. The church's mandate is to proclaim the gospel of the kingdom as evidenced in the ministry of Jesus Christ. As a ministry process, evangelism is the process by which we proclaim the good news of Jesus Christ, which leads a person to salvation.

The ministries of evangelism are variously described in the Bible. All underscore the church and the believer's role in proclaiming the message of salvation that is part and parcel of the gospel. Scripture teaches us to fulfill the great commission (Matthew 28:19-20), preach the gospel (Mark 16:15; 1 Corinthians 15:1-4), to proclaim remission of sin and salvation through Jesus Christ (Luke 24:7; Acts 2:38). Scripture reinforces that salvation comes by the grace of God through our faith in Jesus Christ (Ephesians 2:8). Like Jesus' words to Nicodemus, we are to instruct on the "new birth" (John 3:1-8). We are to pray for and lead unbelievers to repentance and the confession of faith in Jesus (Luke 24:47; Romans 10:9-10). Finally, Scripture reminds us that the Holy Spirit empowers us to be witnesses of Jesus Christ (Acts 1:8).

The ministry of evangelism is critical to the local church—it is the means by which a sinner is transformed into a saint (one who is sanctified or set apart for God's use) and by which the church stays connected to the mission of Jesus in and to the world. In a Church Full of Leaders, evangelism ministries are chartered to intentionally share the gospel with the purpose of converting people to Christ. A Church Full of Leaders will have corporate evangelistic outreach as a church-wide ministry, and it will also encourage congregational members to lead other people to Christ by participating in personal evangelism (sharing, witnessing, and inviting unbelievers to church).

Worship

Believers of the early church gathered together to worship the Lord out of gratefulness, in recognition of His resurrection power, and in response to the active operation of the Holy Spirit in their lives. The New Testament believers expressed their heartfelt reverence in their worship.

In Acts 2:42-47, we see where the believers gathered together in the name of the Lord for exhortation and teaching. They sang praises in the midst of the assembly (Hebrews 2:12) for edification (1 Corinthians 14:26). Privately and collectively, believers sang psalms, hymns, and spiritual songs. The process of worship transforms the heart and strengthens the believer's ongoing relationship with the Lord. Worship ministries are vital to the vibrancy and life of the church.

As in the first church, worship ministries today are those that facilitate our service to God through use of liturgy (praise and worship) and sacraments (baptism and Communion). Worship ministries focus the congregation on magnifying and extolling the Lord with the aim of ushering us into the presence of God and ultimately increasing our sensitivity to the presence of God. In a Church Full of Leaders, every member is charged with leading a life of worship and devotion, publicly and privately, knowing that a leader's public worship will only be as strong as his or her private devotion.

Discipleship

Discipleship ministries are the teaching and instructional ministries of the church aimed at teaching the principles of the faith and enabling believers to live out the profession of their faith in Christ. The core activities of the church that were birthed on the Day of Pentecost show us how critical teaching or discipling converts was to the first church: "and they continued steadfastly in the apostle's doctrine" (Acts 2:42, NKJV).

A disciple is anyone who follows the teachings of a leader. Whereas many people today may espouse the ethical teachings of Jesus, such as "love your neighbor" and "do unto others as you would have them do unto you," a disciple of Christ is a person who follows the very living Word himself, by abiding in His Word (John 8:31), patterning his or her attitude and life after Christ. The process of making disciples, then, is a foundational process that must help people of all ages learn the Word of God, and adhere to the principles that accompany a lifestyle anchored in the teachings of Jesus. Discipleship ministries teach people the principles of the faith, show them how to study the Bible, and equip them to effectively apply the Word to their life situations. These ministries must be led by mature lovers of truth who have themselves been taught to accurately read and interpret Scripture (Acts 13:1; 1 Corinthians 12:28, 29; Ephesians 4:11; 2 Timothy 2:15; Hebrews 5:12; James 3:1).

In a Church Full of Leaders, people from throughout the congregation are equipped to participate in the discipleship process. Teachers are called from the congregation to lead classes (after an appropriate training program) that focus on teaching Bible knowledge and study skills, as well as those that focus on life principles. In a Church Full of Leaders, members are encouraged to study and master the Word to encourage one another, to provide mentoring and coaching of fellow believers. Together teachers and members participate in the leading of teaching ministries that focus the congregation on the Word of God with the aim of creating committed followers of Christ, whose commitment is evidenced in their daily walk.

Fellowship

Shortly after the mass conversion of new believers on the day of Pentecost, the Acts account records that in addition to focusing on the teachings of the apostles, they continued steadfastly in fellowship. This passage thus gives us insight into the necessity of those ministries that help those who start in the faith to continue in the faith.

Fellowship comes from the Greek word *koinonia,* and it means sharing, unity, close association, and partnership. As described by the *Spirit Filled Life Bible, koinonia* "is a unity brought by the Holy Spirit...[that] cements the believers to the Lord Jesus and to each other."[1] The account in Acts helps us

to understand that fellowship included "breaking of bread or sharing common meals, even the Lord's Supper, and praying together." The underlying emphasis was on the common shared experience. The term is variously translated in the New Testament as fellowship, communion, and contribution (1 Corinthians 10:16; Philemon 6,7; Romans 15:26; 2 Corinthians 8:4; Philippians 4:15). Today, as in the New Testament church, fellowship ministries are those ministries that fulfill the biblical notion of *koinonia*—caring for and sharing with one another in such a way that enhances our individual spiritual growth as well as cultivates unity in the congregation. Ministries of fellowship often tend to bring groups of people who have a common demographic affinity together for service, teaching, and socializing. For instance, small-group ministries centered around neighborhood are popular, whereas in other churches ministries for women, ministries for men, ministries for singles, and ministries for married couples are effective ways of ensuring that members are connected to one another in meaningful ongoing ways. In a Church Full of Leaders, people are needed to lead these ministry groups. Leaders must be integrated into the life of the church and facilitate the building of unity within the church.

Service

The term service as a ministry function is both broadly defined and broadly used in the New Testament. From the Greek *diakonia,* the term was used for the religious and spiritual activities associated with preaching and teaching of the Word (Acts 6:4; 20:24; 1 Timothy 1:12), as well as for the practical service of believers in distributing food to widows and making financial contributions (Acts 6:1; Romans 12:7; 2 Corinthians 8:4). Leaders equip the saints for the work of ministry, or service.

Today, as in the New Testament church, leaders balance the ministry of the Word with the ministry of works (or acts of service to and for one another). Service ministries are those ministries that provide support and service to the church as a whole, to the individual members of the church, or to the surrounding communities. Three types of service ministries exist in a Church Full of Leaders: care and support service, administrative service and ministry/service development.

Care and Support Service/Ministries are core to a Church Full of Leaders. Their primary aim is to provide support in carrying out the evangelistic, worship, teaching, and fellowship ministries of the church. Leaders are needed to head support functions that facilitate the smooth operations of other ministry functions. Leaders, both clergy and lay ministers, are needed to lead and facilitate the congregational care ministries.

Administrative and Operations Ministries provide service to that church in terms of governance providing ordering, structuring, and maintenance of the church and its assets.

Service/Ministry Development are those ministries that strengthen the current ministries. These equipping ministries develop and assist with the placement of leaders and workers in ministries, as well as assist in the development of new ministries that help the church fulfill its mission.

Transformative Ministry Definitions—Summary

- **Evangelism Ministries**—Evangelism ministries are chartered to intentionally share the gospel with the purpose of converting people to Christ. A Church Full of Leaders will have corporate evangelistic outreach as a church-wide ministry, and it will also encourage congregational members to participate in personal evangelism (sharing, witnessing, and inviting unbelievers to church).
- **Worship Ministries**—Worship ministries are those that facilitate our service to God through use of liturgy (praise and worship) and sacraments (baptism and Communion). Worship ministries focus the congregation on magnifying and extolling the Lord with the aim of ushering us into the presence of God and ultimately increasing our sensitivity to the presence of God.
- **Discipleship Ministries**—Discipleship ministries are the teaching ministries of the church. These ministries focus the congregation on the Word of God with the aim of creating committed followers of Christ, whose commitment is evidenced in their daily walk
- **Fellowship**—Fellowship ministries are those ministries that fulfill the biblical notion of koinonia–caring for and sharing with one another in such a way that enhances our individual spiritual growth as well as cultivates unity in the congregation. Often ministries of fellowship tend to bring groups of people who have a common demographic affinity together for service, teaching, and socializing.
- **Service Ministries**—Service ministries are those ministries that provide support and service to the church as a whole, to the individual members of the church, or to the surrounding communities.

Transformative ministries are the key operations of a church. Through these ministries people are brought to Christ, built up in their faith, and supported in their growth as they discover their purpose to serve and participate in the work of ministry. As a church grows, more leaders are needed and called forth to participate in the leading of transformative ministries.

A Biblical Model for Organizing and Leading Transformative Ministry

Evangelism	Worship	Discipleship	Fellowship	Service		
				Care & Support Services	**Administration**	**Ministry Development**
Proclaiming the Gospel	Praise, Prayer, Celebration, and Preaching	Facilitating Spiritual Growth through Teaching	Sharing, Caring and Building Relationships & Unity in the Body of Christ	Rendering Support and Helping to Meet Needs	Providing Order, Structure, and Coordination	Developing Current and New Ministries
• Preach the Gospel (Mark 16:15; I Corinthians 15:1-4) • Proclaim remission of sin & salvation through Jesus Christ (Luke 24:47; Acts 2:38) • Proclaim salvation by grace through faith (Ephesians 2:8) • Instruction on the "new birth" (John 3:1-8) • Pray for and lead to repentance and confession of faith (Luke 24:47; Romans 10:9-10) • To be witnesses of Jesus Christ (Acts 1:8) • Proclaiming the Gospel and making disciples (Acts 14:21)	• Gather together in the name of the Lord for exhortation and teaching (Acts 2:42-47; Hebrews 10:25) • Sing praises in the midst of the assembly (Hebrews 2:12) • Sing psalms, hymns and spiritual songs (Ephesians 5:19) • Coming to together in worship for edification (I Corinthians 14:26)	• Make disciples (Matthew 28:19) • Renew the mind (Romans 12:2) • Teaching to abide in the word (John 8:31) • Teaching to be obedient the faith (Acts 6:7) • Exhorting them to continue in the faith (Acts 14:22) • Teaching (I Cor 12:28)	• Develop unity within the Body of Christ (Ephesians 4:13) • Develop relationships and connections within the Body of Christ (Ephesians 4:16) • Fellowship (Acts 4:42) (Koinonia) • Sharing of faith that leads to joy, consolation and refreshing (Philemon 6,7)	• The daily distributions for the widows (Acts 6:1) • Phoebe, who is a servant of the church... she has been a helper of many and of [Paul] (Rom 16:1-2) • Ministry to the hungry, thirsty, naked, homeless, & imprisoned (Matt 25:31-40)	• Selecting and organizing "deacons" for the daily distributions for the widows (Acts 6:3-7) • Facilitation of order (Rom. 12:8; Titus 1:5) • Administration (I Cor 12:28)	• Equipping the Saints for the work of ministry (Eph 4:12) • Release the power and potential (Acts 1:8; Eph 3:20) • Facilitate the discovery of purpose, calling & giftedness (Rom 12:6) • Developing teachers who are responsible and accountable for their influence (James 3:1) • Appointing and developing elders (Acts 14:23)

Figure 7:
A Biblical Model for Organizing and Leading Transformative Ministry

Now that we have laid out a means of organizing transformative ministry, it's time for you to develop a Ministry Matrix for your church. In the Appendix, you will find a sample Church Ministry Matrix, showing how a church could potentially categorize its current ministries. By completing this Ministry Matrix, you will have a better sense of what current ministries are, where you might have gaps, and begin to see how you cluster ministries together for placing and developing leaders. Once completed, your church's Ministry Matrix can be shared with your leaders, congregation, and the public to help people better understand who you are and the ministries comprising your church.

Chapter 5—Reflection

1. Who currently leads the evangelism ministries of your church? How can these ministries be expanded to incorporate more people working toward the evangelistic aims of your church?

2. Who is charged with leading worship at your church? Do worship leaders truly lead people into the presence of God? Is worship a spectator event or a participatory encounter? How do you help leaders translate the encounters of worship into an ongoing lifestyle that is sensitive to the presence and power of God every day?

3. Who is charged with leading the discipleship ministries of your church? Are your discipleship leaders focused on discipling or training others to disciple? Beside classroom instruction, what are additional avenues for developing disciples in your church?

4. Who is charged with leading the fellowship ministries of your church? Are your fellowship leaders focused on connecting members to the church and to each other?

5. Who is charged with leading the service ministries of your church? How do you help your members identify the processes you have in place to help them plug into service?

Who are the people God has called you to serve? Men, women, young adults, children? Poor or prosperous people? People of a specific ethnicity? The church of Jesus Christ is called to minister the love and power of Jesus Christ to all people of all the nations. That is just one thing that distinguishes a church from a specific ministry—churches are formed to accomplish the mission of Jesus to transform people. The transformative ministry processes of the church are intertwined with the mission of the church (see Figure 8).

The Mission of the Church
To make known the manifold wisdom of God (Eph. 3:10)

Evangelism

Worship

To go to all nations and make disciples (Matt. 28:19)

To edify the body of the Christ (Eph. 4:12)

To extend the preaching, teaching & healing ministry of Jesus (Matt. 4:23)

Service

Discipleship

Fellowship

To prevail against the gates of hell (Matt. 16:18)

To the people of the world

Figure 8: The Church's Mission and the Transformative Ministry Process

God calls the church to minister healing, deliverance, and empowerment to men and women, boys and girls of every nation, tribe and tongue, from cradle to grave. There are three types of needs, then, that we must understand in order to lead truly transformative ministry—the universal need for God that all people have, the social and cultural needs associated with the communities that we serve, and the more concrete needs that groups of people with similar characteristics have in common.

The most effective ministries of the church are those that are the most sensitive to the complexity of needs of people—the spiritual, the developmental, and the sociocultural. One framework for us to use in organizing the ministries of a Church Full of Leaders is to identify church-wide ministries that address the universal and sociocultural needs of people and ministries aimed toward people at specific life stages, namely children, teens, and adults. Being able to minister at these three need levels provides us with insight into effective ministry.

(1) The Universal Spiritual Need for God

The universal needs of people might also be called the spiritual needs that are fulfilled by bringing people into a relationship with God through Jesus Christ. These are the needs for salvation, spiritual connection, identity, purpose, and wholeness. The church addresses these needs through a variety of ministries that proclaim the gospel, provide care and healing to broken people, and teach people biblical truth. In order for the church to tap into and address these existential needs, ministry must be revelatory— i.e., the ministry must reveal God's healing and saving virtues to the world God so loves. And though we describe these spiritual needs as universal, they manifest in culturally specific ways. To better understand and, therefore, meet the needs of people, we discern life stages and sociocultural contexts to better develop ministries that meet the diverse needs of the people of the world.

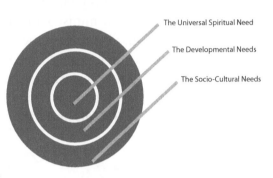

The Universal Spiritual Need

The Developmental Needs

The Socio-Cultural Needs

(2) The Life Stages Needs

All people need God, need to be reconciled to the Father through Jesus Christ, and empowered by the Holy Spirit. Yet people come to the church or the church goes out to find people, who are all at different stages of life. The needs of a child differ from those of a teen, which differ from those of a young adult, which differ from those of a mature adult. Yet the beauty of ministry and the church is that God gifts and equips the servants of God to minister to the needs of people at each life stage. The church must meet people where they are for ministry to stay real.

(3) The Sociocultural Needs

Furthermore, we live in cultural and social contexts that are broken and fragmented, and the church must see the spiritual roots of social maladies and address them as such. Issues such as racism, sexism, and poverty are contextual realities for the church, and the church must address the needs that arise from these conditions if it is to provide relevant ministry to people.

Addressing each of these three levels of needs challenges church leaders to be revelatory, real, and relevant.

Ministry Must be Revelatory. Transformative ministry must reveal the saving, healing, and transforming power of God. Church leaders must be steeped in the Word of

God, taught to meditate on the Word, and develop a prayer-soaked relationship with God so that they are taught to hear God's intentions for transformation.

Ministry Must be Real. Transformative ministry must "keep it real." Churches must establish authentic ministry that is grounded in integrity and deals with real-life stage issues. Leaders must be trained to address issues through transformative programs and processes, integrating the developmental practices to help people grow spiritually, emotionally, intellectually, financially, and relationally.

Ministry Must be Relevant. Churches must make ministry relevant. Ministry must be relevant to the contexts in which people find themselves. Leaders must be taught how to meet people where they are and bring them along to where God wants them to be. That is the heart of transformative leadership. Leaders must be taught to answer the questions people ask, and not offer answers to questions of days gone by. Leaders must be taught to help people solve problems they experience in their daily lives using the timeless principles of the Word of God.

This chapter of the Church Full of Leaders handbook is more hands on than the previous chapters. Its aim is to help you gather information necessary for assessing your current ministry needs. The work of this chapter should be completed by the Church Full of Leaders leadership team.

Developing Your Membership Profiles

There are many survey programs and apps that can be used to understand the makeup of your congregation. Prior to using technology to gather, collect, and report data on your congregation, you must develop an understanding of what you want to learn about your congregation. Following are demographic categories you will want to understand about your congregation:

1. Number of Members

2. Number of Men

3. Number of Women

4. Ethnic/Cultural Backgrounds of the Membership

5. Age

    • Number of members 65+: Seniors/Retirees

    • Number of members 35-64: Middle Age

    • Number of members 25-35: Young Adults

- Number of members 19-24: College-age Students

- Number of members 13-18: Teens

- Number of members 6-12: School-age Children

- Number of members under 5: Preschoolers, Toddlers, and Babies

6.   Education Range

7.   Career/Work/Professional Status

8.   Neighborhood or Zip Code

9.   Socioeconomic Range

10.   Other

For each demographic, construct a pie chart that represents the percentages of your membership in each of the categories. In the space below, write out your reflections on this analysis. What insights did you gain? What do these profiles tell you about the possible needs of the population of people your church fills?
Gender Profile: What does the gender profile suggest about the potential for men's ministry? For women's ministry?

Ethnic/Cultural Profile: What does this profile suggest about the ethnic/cultural diversity in your congregation and surrounding community? What implications does this diversity or homogeneity have for your church's worship? Evangelism? Programs?

Generational Profile: What does this profile suggest about the generational diversity of your congregation and surrounding community? What are the blessings and challenges associated with ministering to Traditionalists, Baby Boomers, Gen Xers, and Millennials? What strategies are needed to reach and engage each generation?

Neighborhood Profile: What is the neighborhood context for your church? Develop a demographic profile for the community in which your church resides. What strategies do you have in place to reach out to your neighborhood or the neighborhood from which your members come? How might your church serve the needs of this neighborhood? How might your church partner with other neighborhood institutions?

Socioeconomics: What economic issues and needs are prevalent in your congregation? What ministry programs might assist congregants in need? What

are the socioeconomic issues associated with the communities in which you serve? How might your congregation meet some of those needs?

Professional/Career/Work Profiles: What does this profile suggest about the employment needs in your congregation? What professionals could you approach to volunteer to develop a career-focused ministry to assist members in the congregation with job development, re-entry, resume building, interviewing, and so on? Or what professionals could be enlisted to lead other specific ministries such as health, financial, legal, IT?

Ministry Assessment

Examine your ministry plan for each demographic, and for each group ask yourself, "Is our ministry revelatory, real, and relevant?" If not, what changes need to be made to your ministry?

	Revelatory Word-Based	Real Developmentally Appropriate	Relevant Contextually Appropriate
Women			
Men			
Young Adults			
Teens			
Children			

Reviewing the Needs of Ministry Populations

We can develop effective ministry plans when we fully understand the needs of the people we serve. Following are seven steps for identifying the needs of each demographic group in your church:

1. Form a team charged with developing a process and guidelines for ministry leaders to understand the needs of their ministry population.
2. Understand the demographics and needs of each ministry population.
3. Use surveys and questionnaires to query members about issues that affect them.
4. Hold conversations with ministry members.
5. Listen to requests that are given by ministry members.
6. Conduct focus groups of population members to explore needs and ministry ideas.
7. For youth ministry, develop protocols for conducting background checks for all youth workers and developing guidelines for child protection procedures.

The most effective ministry occurs when the gifts and passions of people of God intersect with the needs of the people of the world.

Chapter 6—Reflection

1. How do your church's ministries meet people where they are?

2. Do your ministries offer programs that meet the varied needs of believers within your congregation no matter what stage they are in life?

3. Consider how revelatory, real, and relevant your ministries are. Then consider ways you can strengthen them if they are lagging in some way.

4. Consider one of the following ministry groups in your church: men, women, youth, singles, married couples, community group. Now think about the unique needs of that group. Think about what your ministry currently looks like and write down ways you can improve the ministry to make it more...

   Revelatory:

   Real:

   Relevant:

More and more churches of all sizes are using a combination of paid and unpaid staff to deliver ministry. Small to medium-sized churches especially need to attend to organizing structure in order to support the expansion of ministry programs, which in turn help meet more people's needs. As a result, church leaders need an effective ministry structure by which to organize the leaders at every level.

Church Size and Structure

Dr. Timothy Keller, in his article "Leadership and Church Size Dynamics: How Strategy Changes with Growth," provides great insight into the challenges and opportunities for moving a church through the various thresholds of growth. He provides some definitions of size that we have adapted for the Church Full of Leaders process.

Small Church—up to 200 members

Medium Church—200-1000 members

Large Church—1000 – 2000 members

Mega Church—2000+ members[1]

A small church often starts off with a founding pastor (or co-pastors) who is visionary and/or charismatic and who attracts members to the church based on dynamic preaching, insightful teaching, or connected relationships. The church has great potential but will stagnate if it does not put a leadership structure in place that facilitates the 1) ministering (not just preaching) to more than what a single pastor can reach, 2) placement and development of leaders to support and align members with the church vision, and 3) a mechanism for plugging new members into the ministry.

In a small church, the leadership structure will entail the solo pastor (or co-pastors) and leaders over ministries that are small but have great potential for growth. This might entail a pastor who preaches on Sunday, teaches Bible study, provides pastoral care; a small praise team; and teachers for one or two discipleship groups (perhaps Sunday school or women's and men's classes). As the church grows, new teachers will be identified, a youth ministry may be formed, a new member orientation will be established, and the worship ministry expanded. This growth requires more leadership and provides an opportunity for more people to become plugged into the church.

Yet as the church continues to grow, the complexity of the church increases and the more defined the leadership structure needs to become. It is at this point where ministry teams need to be developed and trained and leaders identified for these small groups. According to Keller,

> "In smaller churches, classes and groups can be larger because virtually everyone in the church is cared for directly by full-time trained ministry staff, each of whom can care for 50–200 people. In larger churches, however, the internal groupings need to be smaller, because people are cared for by lay shepherds, each of whom can care for 10–20 people if given proper supervision and support. Thus in a larger church, the more small groups you have per 100 people in attendance, the better cared for people are and the faster the church grows."[2]

Unfortunately, many small churches are not led even by a full-time trained pastor; yet this reality makes Keller's point even more salient. These pastors have an even smaller span of care, and the need to enlist more members into the leadership processes of the church are even more urgent. Indeed, as the church grows, the need for leaders at every level grows.

Leadership Roles—The Building Blocks of Structure

To some people, a Church Full of Leaders sounds like a church with all leaders and no followers—or a church with no clearly defined leadership roles. Nothing could be further from the truth. A Church Full of Leaders depends on more members of the congregation accepting a call to lead, by being properly trained and prepared to serve in an expanding array of leadership roles. The Church Full of Leaders process identifies five levels of leadership competence within the local church.

L1—Ministry Team Member. The first level entails personal leadership that all maturing members attain to in their own personal and spiritual growth. Operating from a sense of call, identification with the ministry, or desire to give back, these members serve on ministry teams and are thus introduced to the leadership process. As members of the team they are participating in the church's leadership process and helping to advance the goals and aims of the ministry. These people may be new to ministry leadership and show great interest in and willingness to serve and become part of a ministry. In so doing, they become a part of the leadership process of the ministry. They may get involved by leading tasks or projects within a ministry. This "leadership" entails the demonstration of task completion with high standards of excellence and leading projects or assignments on a ministry team.

L2–Team/Small Group Leader or Class Leader. This is the role of leading a team of people, small group ministry or class. Team leaders must demonstrate the spiritual maturity to lead a team of people in line with the vision and aims of the ministry of which they are a part. These leaders work to build and guide their own ministry team in order to accomplish the overall goals of the ministry. These leaders become a critical link in ensuring the members of the team are fitly joined together (Ephesians 4:16) or connected to the ministry teams. L2 leaders are critical to every size church, and these leaders play a crucial front-line role with helping members stay connected to the church.

L3–Ministry Leadership. This is the role of leading a ministry that entails teams of teams. A ministry is nothing more than a team of teams. A person who leads an entire ministry within the church has responsibility to align that ministry with the pastoral or church-wide vision, develop ministry tactics for his or her ministry, develop leaders within the ministry to accomplish the goals and objectives of the ministry, build and maintain the ministry organization or infrastructure to support the work of their ministry and at the same time align and collaborate with other ministry leaders for the overall work of the church. It is crucial for a ministry leader to lead the ministry with a leadership team and recognize she or he is a leader of leaders. In small churches, the pastor wears many hats and may lead ministries such as the women's ministry or men's ministry, but will need to prayerfully identify people who can be developed to lead these ministries. The L3 leadership level is crucial as a church transitions from small to medium and ministries become more complex.

L4–Department Leadership. The role of leading multiple ministries in the church that consists of both paid and volunteer staff. These multiple ministries cluster together to comprise a ministry department. The L4 leadership level is crucial as a church transitions from medium to large, where it becomes necessary to have a mechanism that brings similar ministries together for development, training, and coordination of ministry services.

L5–Church-wide Leadership. The role of leading the entire church or large portions of the church falls to the pastor or pastoral team. These leaders provide the spiritual and organizational direction for the church and leaders, develop the infrastructure for the entire church, develop the leaders of the church, and provide the overarching mechanisms for galvanizing all the ministries to fulfill the God-given purpose for their particular church.

Even after ministry procedures are put in place, many churches need a coherent structure to provide the reporting relationships and accountability. Each church will develop a structure that fits its strategy, as the old adage states, "Form follows function." One place to start for leaders who desire to build a

Church Full of Leaders is to structure the ministry departments and teams around the five transformational ministry processes of the church discussed throughout this handbook. Focusing on the transformative ministry processes provides a functional approach to developing your organizational structure, allowing the ministry leaders to define the needs of the ministry before placing people into the functions. To build your leadership structure, you will want to follow these principles:

- Commit to developing members who are faithful disciples of Jesus Christ. As they grow in the grace and knowledge of our Lord Jesus Christ, they begin to live out biblical principles in the various dimensions of their lives. Through the Word of God and the Holy Spirit, they are transformed bit by bit, walking out their faith in their homes, at work, in the neighborhood daily. This at its core is strong discipleship—the effect of the believer's life upon those with whom she or he comes into contact as a witness and light of the love of Jesus.

- Train individuals to become proficient in an area of ministry by diligently fulfilling their ministry assignments in a spirit of excellence, in a timely manner, and with an attitude of love and service. In this way, individuals serving in ministry are fulfilling the basic leadership requirements of L1 leaders. Train them to follow and be accountable to the leaders who have responsibility for the ministry team on which they serve.

- Prayerfully select members of team ministry to serve based on gifting, experience, training, preparation for appropriate leadership levels and responsibility, and faithfulness to previous ministry tasks.

- Ensure that every ministry team has a leader (L2). Very rarely are there individual contributors in a church—those not serving on a ministry team or with other members to accomplish some tasks of ministry or reporting to a senior ministry leader. With few exceptions, individuals doing ministry on their own are not aligned to a core ministry function or process of the church. They will feel disconnected, may be left out of communication loops, and may ultimately feel overworked and isolated.

- Develop a role description for each ministry leadership position so leaders are clear on their responsibilities and the expectations of them. Every ministry team should have a clear purpose, targeted audience, and clear roles.

- Group similar ministry teams together and provide a common ministry leader (L3). Make sure ministry team leaders who serve within the same function are accountable to a ministry function.

- Group similar ministries together to form a department and provide a common leader (L4). Make sure ministry leaders who serve within the same function are accountable to a department leader. Make sure leaders hold regular meetings for sharing church-wide leadership information, for communicating department or functional goals, for intra-departmental coordination, and for building a cohesive and unified department/function.

When developing a leadership infrastructure, it is wise to keep leadership roles for your size church in mind, customizing the core training for each level of leadership. See Figure 9a for a small church (where pastor and members wear multiple hats) and Figure 9b for a medium-sized church (where more members have been enlisted into the process of leadership). In chart 9b, keep in mind until more leaders are identified and equipped, individuals may serve in multiple leadership roles. Chart 9c completes our sample organization by providing a prototype structure for a leadership team of a connecting ministry.

Leadership Competencies[3]

It is helpful for pastoral leaders to identify the set of competencies that are necessary to be successful in your church. Leadership competencies are the constellation of skills required for a particular leadership role. For ministry

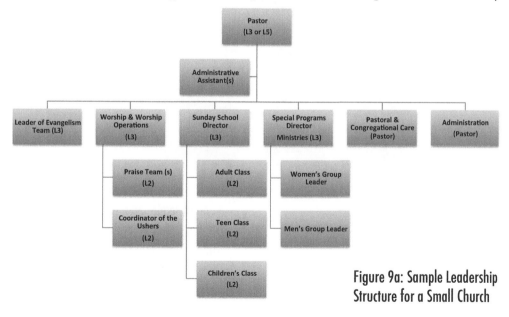

Figure 9a: Sample Leadership Structure for a Small Church

Figure 9b: Sample Leadership Chart for a Medium-Sized Church

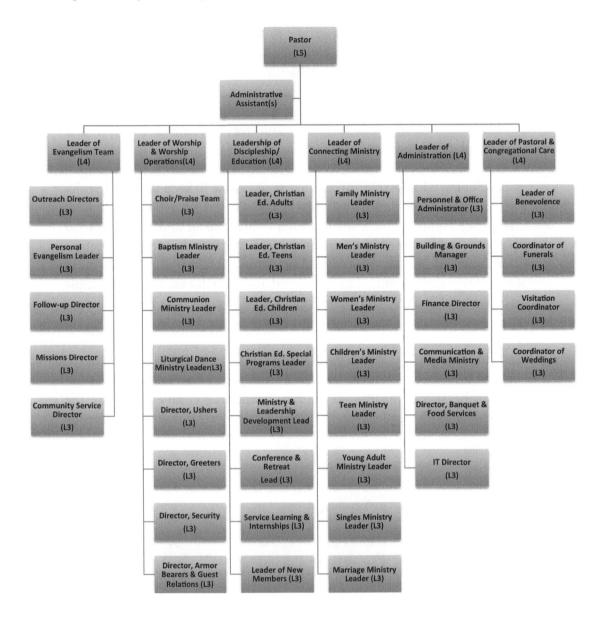

*An L4 leader on this chart may be a pastor, minister, or director. The specific title will depend on the culture of a given church.

Figure 9c: Sample Leadership Chart for a Connecting Ministry

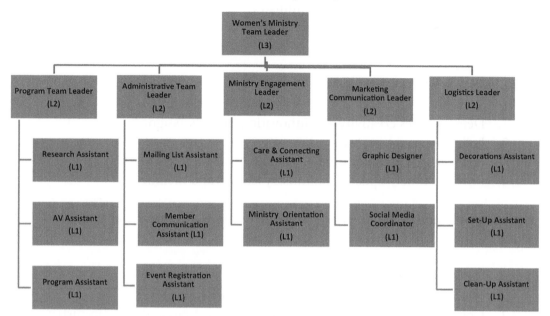

leaders, competencies must be spiritual, cognitive, and behavioral. Clearly articulating leadership competencies helps us prayerfully select leaders for a given role, identify training needs for people in the roles, and provide performance feedback to those serving in the role. Competencies provide a framework for developing leaders for a particular context. These skills are necessary for the leadership roles to which they are attached. When looking to place people into these roles, these are the competencies the people must be able to demonstrate or be trained and developed in. Following are examples of these leadership competencies for ministry:

L1 – Ministry Team Member

Maturing Spiritual Walk–demonstrates spiritual growth and qualities of a maturing leader

1. Consistently practices spiritual disciplines such as Bible reading and prayer
2. Consistently gives of their time, talent, and tithe
3. Maintains a biblical lifestyle and uses the Word to guide his or her choices
4. Attends and participates in corporate prayer, worship, and Bible study

Willingness to Assume Ministry Responsibility

1. Demonstrates faithfulness to ministry
2. Conveys interest, calling, or passion to the ministry
3. Follows ministry leadership

Shows Initiative in Ministry Responsibilities

1. Demonstrates creativity and innovation in tasks assigned
2. Follows through on tasks assigned
3. Follows up with other ministry members to complete tasks
4. Provides timely updates to ministry leaders and members

Organization–demonstrates the mastery of one or more organizational leadership skills

1. Serves effectively on a ministry team
2. Follows through on projects or tasks that are started
3. Consistently demonstrates promptness to meetings and other ministry activities
4. Able to organize agendas or lesson plans

L2–Team/Small Group, Team, or Class Leaders

L2 leaders need to be proficient or be trained in the competencies listed in L1, as well as the following:

Communication–the ability to effectively convey ministry information and plans orally and in writing to a variety of constituents, including staff, ministry leaders, and volunteers

1. Effectively and clearly communicates the strategic and tactical objectives and plans to appropriate parties
2. Maintains a tracking system for tactical objectives/plans to limit miscommunication
3. Communicates with candor in a manner in which information can be received positively and with consistency across various functions of responsibility

Interpersonal Leadership–the ability to demonstrate interpersonal competence that builds trust and enhances interpersonal relationships in ministry

1. Listens well to others, non-defensively and with openness to hear the heart of issues
2. Maintains confidentiality
3. Communicates and conveys ideas and thoughts clearly
4. Gives and receives feedback
5. Resolves conflict biblically

Spiritual Leadership—demonstrates a commitment to spiritual growth and facilitating the spiritual growth of others; the ability to set the spiritual tone for the ministry and provide the type of leadership that inspires through consistent modeling of spiritual disciplines and practice, both public and private

1. Demonstrates Word-based faith and is faithful
2. Is sensitive and in tune with the Holy Spirit, as well as his or her own interior life
3. Lives out of a clear or (growing) sense of purpose
4. Exhibits godly character as evident in his or her attitudes and actions
5. Leads with and in love—demonstrates care and compassion toward others
6. Demonstrates unity
7. Lives a biblically defined holy life
8. Demonstrates wisdom in decision making

Ministry Proficiency or Gifting—demonstrates a proficiency or gifting in a specific area of ministry, such as teaching, audio-visual, food services, health education, and so on

1. Has skills in a specific administrative or ministry area
2. Demonstrates capable gifting for service, including helps
3. Demonstrates faithfulness in serving, using skills and gifts
4. Demonstrates willingness/initiative to serve, using skills and gifts

L3—Leaders of A Ministry Team or Program Team
L3 Leaders need the competencies listed for L1 and L2 as well as the following:

Program Leadership—the ability to execute or implement ministry programs, projects, or interventions that align with the pastor's vision; demonstrates the ability to follow a framework for a new or existing ministry or education program, project, or service

1. Has experience, knowledge, and familiarity with Bible, spiritual

formation, and/or Christian education development principles and practices, and demonstrates the ability to translate those principles into effective curricula and ministry programs

2. Develops or contributes toward the improvement of programs that go beyond the status quo and moves the ministry team to a new level
3. Has the ability to engage appropriate people and gain buy-in to ministry programs
4. Maintains and tracks ministry budget

Teamwork–the ability to build and effectively lead ministry teams to accomplish ministry and program objectives

1. Partners effectively with other departments to implement ministry programs effectively
2. Partners effectively with ministry leaders to develop and implement ministry programs successfully
3. Follows and assists ministry leadership with administrative processes

Meeting Leadership–the ability to run effective meetings to disseminate information to the department or ministry team, as well as bring teams together to maintain cohesiveness and build unity around common goals

1. Effectively plans meetings and notifies department of meeting objectives in advance
2. Effectively uses meeting tools such as agendas and minutes to maintain departmental communication
3. Effectively utilizes the resources of other departmental meetings to hold productive and fruitful meetings

L4 Leaders (Leaders of Multiple Ministry Teams or Department)

L4 Leaders need the competencies listed for L1, L2, L3 as well as the following:

Organizational Leadership–the ability to build and effectively lead multiple ministry teams to accomplish departmental objectives; able to develop both ministry programmatic objectives and organizational/operational objectives, educational programs, projects, or interventions that align with the pastor's vision; helps to move the congregation foward

1. Demonstrates the ability to systematically develop and articulate a framework for a new or existing program, project, or process
2. Has the ability to engage appropriate people and gain buy-in to ministry strategy

3. Partners effectively with other ministry departments to implement ministry programs effectively
4. Follows and assists ministry leadership with administrative processes
5. Develops and manages departmental budget

L5 Leaders—Senior Most Leaders/Pastoral Leaders[4]

L5 Leaders need the competencies listed for L1, l2, L3, L4 as well as the following:

Strategic Development—the ability to develop ministry programs, projects, or interventions that align with the pastor's vision; helps to move the congregation toward the pastoral vision; and/or innovatively meets the needs of specific groups within the church. Strategic development also includes the development of departmental leaders, ministry leaders, and team leaders

1. Demonstrates the ability to systematically develop and articulate a framework for a new or existing ministry program, project, or service
2. Has experience, knowledge, and familiarity with Bible, spiritual formation, pastoral leadership, and/or leadership development principles and practices, and demonstrates the ability to translate those principles into effective ministry
3. Develops or contributes toward the development of innovative programs that go beyond the status quo and moves the church toward the vision
4. Has the ability to engage appropriate people and gain buy-in to ministry strategies

Pastoral Leadership—the ability to lead a church or a major function of a church by casting vision, and providing oversight to the spiritual and administrative processes of the entire church and its ministries

1. Demonstrates the ability to systematically develop and articulate a framework for a new or existing ministry program, project, or service
2. Has experience, knowledge, and familiarity with Bible, spiritual formation, pastoral leadership, and/or leadership development principles and practices, and demonstrates the ability to translate those principles into effective ministry
3. Develops or contributes toward the development of innovative programs that go beyond the status quo and moves the church toward the vision
4. Has the ability to engage appropriate people and gain buy-in to ministry strategies

Role or Position Descriptions

What is often the case, especially in growing churches, is one individual will have responsibility for multiple functions or roles. It is imperative that the expectations for these roles are clearly articulated. A role description can help pastoral leaders clearly articulate the scope and function of a particular role or position.

As mentioned before, what will determine the level of leadership needed to lead specific functions within your church structure will be the size and complexity of the church and its leadership staff. Sometimes called position descriptions, these formal expectations summarize the position, reporting/accountability structure, state the responsibilities of the leadership position or role, and articulate the set of competencies needed to effectively fulfill the role.

Figure 10: Position Description Template

POSITION TITLE: _____

REPORTS TO:_____

JOB SUMMARY

Provide a 2-3 sentence description of this position

ESSENTIAL FUNCTIONS

Provide 5-7 bullet points of the key responsibilities of this position.

COMPETENCIES

Identify the essential competencies related to the appropriate level of leadership necessary to successfully perform the functions of this position. Starting with Level 1 leaders, leaders at every level will be expected to demonstrate more competencies. It is essential to commit to ongoing development of leaders in order to develop a Church Full of Leaders.

See the appendix for position description templates for L1-L5 positions.

Next, pastoral leaders must clearly identify the responsibilities associated with particular roles/positions. These responsibilities must include the essential functions of the position such as managing volunteer leaders, developing programs, and coordinating youth activities.

Finally, the position description should clearly identify the reporting and accountability relationships, so paid and volunteer staff members know to whom they are responsible and by whom they will be held accountable. Following is a template for writing position descriptions:

Closing

Just as the skeleton provides the structure of the body, roles, competencies, role descriptions, reporting relationships and responsibilities provide the structure for effective ministry. Clear leadership roles and responsibilities are the hallmark of a Church Full of Leaders.

Chapter 7 – Reflections

1. How clear is your current structure? How might organizing according to the transformative ministry process help bring more order to your church?

2. How does having clear position descriptions help you plug people into ministry leadership?

So how do we engage more members into ministry and eventually help them to embrace their role in the leadership processes of the church? What tends to happen is we attract the same people into major ministry processes and eventually run the risk of burning out or losing the few, the proud, and the "chosen"!

What is needed is a formal process for "recruiting" new volunteers, or uncovering those gifts and talents that lie dormant in the pews. A formal process not only helps leaders identify and place new servants beyond the same 20 percent who always serve, but it also helps leaders identify and discern future leaders.

Shifting Thinking, Changing Culture

When members are asked to volunteer for ministry assignments, they may have a tendency to approach those assignments as optional—one of many things on their busy, already full plates. They may feel, "If I don't feel like showing up, I don't have to." If something more important arises, I must attend to that first. Obviously, ministries can be impacted in a negative way when the people ministry leaders rely upon approach their ministry assignments with such a perspective. Too often, someone drops the ball and as a result, a service is not rendered and a message is not conveyed. And some church volunteers view their roles just as that: optional. If a person isn't paid to do something, he or she doesn't always feel obligated to show up, especially if something else comes up in his or her life. However, we can help members who "volunteer" begin to see their roles differently by helping them to view themselves as stakeholders in the ministry.

Whether it's greeting someone at the door on Sunday morning, organizing hymnals for worship services, serving cookies and punch during social hour, or taking attendance in a Sunday school class—if they can see what they do and how they do as integral to the purpose of ministry, they may see their roles differently. More than volunteers with options who were recruited by fellow parishioners, they will see themselves as servants called by God and committed to doing their part to carry out the work of the ministry. These servants are truly L1 or L2 leaders and are the pipeline for identifying and placing more leaders.

The work of ministry is vast and the aim of the church is to extend the ministry of Jesus Christ in word, worship, sacrament, and service. Sometimes members mistakenly or naively believe that those called to preach or teach do the real work of ministry. Yet Scripture reminds us that believers who respond to the call to serve in any capacity are mission critical. Consider the following passage:

Now in those days, when the number of the disciples was multiplying, there arose a complaint against the Hebrews by the Hellenists, because their widows were neglected in the daily distribution. Then the twelve summoned the multitude of the disciples and said, "It is not desirable that we should leave the word of God and serve tables. Therefore, brethren, seek out from among you seven men of good reputation, full of the Holy Spirit and wisdom, whom we may appoint over this business; but we will give ourselves continually to prayer and to the ministry of the word." And the saying pleased the whole multitude. And they chose Stephen, a man full of faith and the Holy Spirit, and Philip, Prochorus, Nicanor, Timon, Parmenas, and Nicolas, a proselyte from Antioch, whom they set before the apostles; and when they had prayed, they laid hands on them. Then the word of God spread, and the number of the disciples multiplied greatly in Jerusalem, and a great many of the priests were obedient to the faith. Acts 6:1-7, NKJV

As the body of Christ grew, so did the needs among the people. Instead of adding on to their primary assignment to preach and teach God's Word, the apostles called a meeting of the disciples and had them to choose seven men who would be willing to serve food to the poor among the believers. Those seven men were then formally anointed and commissioned by the apostles to serve food.

On the surface, serving food may not seem like such a big deal, but it was important enough for the apostles to pray for the men assigned to do it, which tells us that we shouldn't take lightly any area of service. In part, because of those men's response to the call to serve and dedication to the task before them, God's Word flourished and the body of Christ continued to grow. "But you are a chosen generation, a royal priesthood, a holy nation, His own special people, that you may proclaim the praises of Him who called you out of darkness into His marvelous light" (1 Peter 2:9, NKJV). The word "chosen" comes from the Greek *eklektos,* which means believers were picked, gathered for a special service and privileges. More than carrying out a task, we are called to service to glorify God and to live out the gospel. *The Life Application Bible* notes about the seven men assigned to serve the poor, "By caring for these powerless people, the church put God's Word into practice."[1] Likewise, when we serve, we put God's Word into practice.

No matter how small a task may seem, servants should not take their assignments lightly; they must take them seriously, to the point of consecrating themselves for service (preparing their hearts and minds, being reminded of why they serve—to help spread the gospel, to edify God's people, to glorify God).

A Biblical Call to Serve

"Go therefore and make disciples of all the nations" ~Matthew 28:19a, NKJV

Volunteering is an option, but serving is not. Jesus commissioned every believer to service. In fact, understanding the root words of each helps us to really appreciate the differences. *Merriam-Webster* defines a volunteer as a person who voluntarily undertakes (based on one's own choice) or expresses a willingness to undertake a service. "Volunteer" and "voluntary" stem from the Latin and French words that mean "of one's free will," and initiated with military service as men of their own free will or volition enlisted in the armed services to protect their country.

Clearly, volunteerism is laudable, yet for ministry perhaps the word has lost some sense of call and duty when it comes to the work of ministry. Servant and service, on the other hand, are defined by that same dictionary as one who serves others, especially one that performs duties about the person or home of a master or personal employer. In fact, in the New Testament, servant and service are translated from the Greek *diakaneo,* which means to "attend, or wait upon." The word carried with it the notion of supplying the necessities of life, providing care of the poor or sick. It is the same word from which we get the administration of the office of deacon, but it is not limited to that office. As followers of Christ, we are servants of Jesus Christ, our master. Or as the apostle Paul more aptly stated, "servants" "chosen by God to be _____" (Romans 1:1, KJV). For Paul, that blank was filled with apostle. For us is it might be usher, choir member, greeter, teacher, and so on. No matter what role we're called to fill, we are servants to Christ. Whereas volunteerism entails giving of one's own will, serving entails following God's will! Think about it: Service to God's kingdom is not optional. Our service—and how we serve—*is* Christianity in action. In a Church Full of Leaders, our goal is to link the request to volunteer with the call to serve!

When we call on believers to serve, we may emphasize that fundamental call, as well as the benefits and blessings that result when they respond to God's call. God's kingdom grows. As leaders, we can help members see that when they decide to serve, using their talent and time, the church grows, people come to know the Lord and other believers grow in their faith. Needs are met. Meeting the basic needs of others, such as providing food and clothing through an outreach ministry, spreads God's love; it shows others that God loves them and knows what they need. Spiritual growth occurs. Growing in faith doesn't just occur in a Sunday school class, a Bible study, or during personal times of devotion. It also occurs when believers are living out the Word by way of serving (Galatians 5:13). Growth occurs when servants build relationships of accountability with each other and they feel like part of a family.

A Comprehensive and Systematic Approach to Growing Our Servant Base

Developing a formal process for building the number of believers who serve is critical for effectively moving more members from being Sunday morning saints only to becoming active servants who use their gifts to carry out the church's mission. The process may include the following:

- a systematic way for collecting initial data (e.g., a recruitment card or application)
- sharing the available opportunities (e.g., an orientation or one-on-one interview)
- assessing gifts and skills (e.g., a spiritual gifts inventory and skills inventory)
- placement (e.g., matching the servant with a ministry)
- retention (e.g., follow-up meetings or ongoing training)

The process may be different for each church, as the culture and size of the church determines what features are necessary and, thus, helps to shape what the process looks like.

In a Church Full of Leaders, ministry leaders come together and prayerfully develop a formal system—something that can be maintained and further developed electronically—for ongoing recruitment. In churches that have a formal servanthood ministry, the leader of that ministry would take the lead on such a project. In that case, it may be helpful for that leader to not only engage the team of servants who support that ministry, but also to garner input from the ministry leads of the various auxiliaries.

Of course, after creating a process, leaders must implement the process. For churches that do not use a servanthood/service engagement ministry as a central base for recruitment, leaders may need to identify an administrative servant or two who can help manage the process that has been developed. Depending on the size of your team, this person may even help to develop forms and databases needed for tracking information about each servant (e.g., name, age, membership status, results from assessments, placement). This is particularly important for following through every step, as it can improve placement and retention. Calls for new servants are often placed without follow up or follow through, which causes those believers to feel as though they are not really needed. When a member does not feel needed in his or her church, it can lead to a bad feeling about the church overall, particularly if the member is new to the faith. In the worst case, the member may leave the church. So it is critical that as leaders we honor the processes we develop and implement for recruiting new servants and developing future leaders. While placement and retention is a two-way street, leaders must diligently follow through on recruitment and

placement efforts—they must demonstrate genuine care for those who serve that goes beyond the work they do for the ministry, as discipleship involves building relationship.

As with any new thing, leaders will likely have to make adjustments to the process once they learn what works and what does not work in recruiting and placing believers into service. Once we've figured it out, we should always look for ways to enhance and expand the process, especially as our churches grow.

Penetrating the Pews

The law of the vital few (also known as the 80-20 rule or Pareto Principle) states that approximately 80 percent of the effects come from 20 percent of the cause.[2] In our conversation, that translates to 20 percent of servants doing 80 percent of the work, or the same people doing the work all the time. So how can we begin to get around the same 20 percent of members who respond to the call to serve and begin penetrating the pews, where so many talents lie dormant? Leaders can use a mix of traditional methods and new technology to not only recruit and retain but also to develop systems that work for their churches.

Recruitment Campaigns. Bulletin and pulpit announcements are common vehicles for recruiting believers to serve; yet, one organization considers this "old fashioned tool" and other traditional methods as somewhat archaic and ineffective.[3] Leaders, however, must consider that each person is different. How they communicate and receive information will be different; therefore, every method can be effective. Knowing our audience and considering new ways to use old vehicles of communication can achieve our goal. For example, being strategic and intentional about the language we use in an announcement can prove effective in drawing not only enough people but also those whom God has called to serve in that specific area. For example, if we are seeking women to work on ministry teams in our women's ministry, instead of our announcement reading this way:

> *The Women's Ministry is seeking new volunteers. If you're good at marketing, event planning, or organizing, plan to attend our informational this Wednesday, September 4, at 6:30 p.m., or stop by the information booth after today's service for more information.*

It could read this way:

> *Who knows a woman's heart better than another woman? The Women's Ministry is calling all women with a heart for serving their sisters in Christ. Join our leadership team Wednesday, September*

4, before Bible class at 6:30 p.m., to learn how you can help us carry out life-changing ministry that impacts the life of women at Community Church. If you're good at marketing, event planning, and organizing, that's great—but every talent is needed. If you cannot attend Wednesday's meeting, stop by the information booth after today's service to sign up.

Fairs. Hosting a recruitment fair is an effective way to move dormant members from the pews to service. In large churches, the servanthood or ministry engagement ministry typically organizes and hosts the fair, working with auxiliary leaders to ensure all ministry groups are represented. If your church does not have such a ministry, you and other ministry leaders can come together and plan the event. In addition to putting more gifts to work, it is a great way to introduce members (including those who serve already) to auxiliaries and ministry groups they are unfamiliar with and help them understand how the groups help carry out the overall mission of the church. Determine how often you want to hold the fair (one to two times a year is recommended), what the fair will entail, the best time to hold it (e.g., what is the best day to capture those who have never served before?), what you want participants to walk away with, and how you plan to follow up to ensure everyone who signed up to serve is eventually placed.

Technology. Church leaders must consider the effectiveness of Internet technology for not only recruiting more believers but also for retaining those new servants once they've been placed. There are low-cost and no-cost technologies, like Churchvolunteercentral.com, designed specifically to help churches improve their recruitment efforts. Leaders can also utilize their church Web sites to recruit and build their servant base. For instance, the Web site can be developed to allow believers in your church to search and apply for service opportunities in your church, as well as receive feedback. A large church in Memphis, Tennessee, once provided a gifts assessments survey on its Web site to help believers identify areas in which they would best serve.[4] Utilizing low-cost online resources, such as Churchvolunteercentral.com, is a great way for leaders to access the tools they need to recruit and retain new volunteers, or to research how to create such tools themselves. They provide tips, training, and tools (e.g., spiritual gift assessments, background checks, forms, and templates) for creating databases, reports, and so on that will help us with follow-up, follow-through, and retention.

New Member Orientations. Most churches conduct new member orientations. Such sessions provide an excellent setting for teaching the importance of serving in the church and the expectation that every member will seek their place. Being

new to the faith or the church (in the case of one simply transferring his or her membership) is often accompanied with excitement and eagerness. It is important as leaders that we stress that the expectation that they serve is not ours as much as it is God's. He not only calls them to salvation but to serve. However, it is also important that new believers understand that there are areas in which they can immediately begin serving (e.g., serving food in the kitchen or for special events) and areas in which they must first be spiritually prepared to serve. So there are three things that should be stressed to new members about service: They are first called to salvation, they are called to serve the Kingdom in a specific way, and God will prepare them to carry out that specific call. The conversion and call of the apostle Paul is a good example to share. He was on one mission—to persecute and shut down the church—when the Lord stopped him in his tracks and set him on the path He had ordained for him:

> Then Saul, still breathing threats and murder against the disciples of the Lord, went to the high priest and asked letters from him to the synagogues of Damascus, so that if he found any who were of the Way, whether men or women, he might bring them bound to Jerusalem. As he journeyed he came near Damascus, and suddenly a light shone around him from heaven. Then he fell to the ground, and heard a voice saying to him, "Saul, Saul, why are you persecuting Me?" And he said, "Who are You, Lord?" Then the Lord said, "I am Jesus, whom you are persecuting. It is hard for you to kick against the goads." So he, trembling and astonished, said, "Lord, what do You want me to do?" Then the Lord said to him, "Arise and go into the city, and you will be told what you must do." (Acts 9:1-6, NKJV)

Our salvation and our specific call to serve are ordained by God; we were chosen by God before the foundation of the world to glorify Him with our lives and our service (Ephesians 1:3-6). The apostle Paul had a different agenda when the Lord called him to salvation; however, he immediately answered the call, and the Lord told Him there was a specific assignment for him. The Lord then enlisted another believer, Ananias, to help prepare Paul.

> Now there was a certain disciple at Damascus named Ananias; and to him the Lord said in a vision, "Ananias." And he said, "Here I am, Lord." So the Lord said to him, "Arise and go to the street called Straight, and inquire at the house of Judas for one called Saul of Tarsus, for behold, he is praying. And in a vision he has seen a man named Ananias coming in and putting his hand on him, so that he might receive his sight." (Acts 9:10-12, NKJV)

The next verses reveal Ananias's skepticism.

"Lord, I have heard from many about this man, how much harm he has done to Your saints in Jerusalem. And here he has authority from the chief priests to bind all who call on Your name."

But the Lord told Ananias that it was okay because Paul was "a chosen vessel of Mine to bear My name before Gentiles, kings, and the children of Israel." Ananias obeyed and went to where Paul was. "And Ananias went his way and entered the house; and laying his hands on him he said, "Brother Saul, the Lord Jesus, who appeared to you on the road as you came, has sent me that you may receive your sight and be filled with the Holy Spirit." Immediately there fell from his eyes something like scales, and he received his sight at once; and he arose and was baptized." Notice the laying on of hands here, just as the apostles lay hands on the deacons before they began serving the poor? In the New Testament, the laying on of hands signified a number of things, including the bestowal of blessings and benediction (Matthew 19:15); the restoration of health (Matthew 9:18); the reception of the Holy Spirit in baptism (Acts 8:17, 19); the gifts and rights of an office (Acts 6:6; 13:3; 2 Timothy 1:6). [5]

In this example, Ananias is a leader in the church helping to disciple a new believer. When we call members out of the pews and into service, we are engaging in discipleship, showing them what it means to live for Christ via service. That's why developing formal recruitment processes that are strategic in drawing and developing new servants is critical to our overall purpose as a church: to glorify God through the spreading of the gospel and the building up of His people. Once we put out the call, get the response, and follow through, we must help new servants identify their gifts and how best to use them for the building of the kingdom.

Spiritual Gifts

One vehicle to help members become engaged in ministry is an assessment to help them discover their spiritual gifts. For believers, discovering their spiritual gifts can help unlock the secrets of their purpose, as well as help them understand and accept the distinct ways in which God has gifted them to serve and perhaps lead.

People who serve according to their distinct giftedness serve with passion and purpose. They are clear on the gifts God has entrusted to them and endowed them with. Yet every believer may not be clear on their own giftedness. Discovering and using their spiritual gifts is a process, and leaders in a Church Full of Leaders can use a spiritual gifts framework as one vehicle to help engage members into service.

Stemming from the Greek words or derivatives *pneuma(tikos)* and *charisma(ta)*, spiritual gifts are Spirit *(pneuma)* gifts *(charismata)*. Sometimes the Greek text uses *pneumatikos* (1 Corinthians 12:1, 14:1, 12); and other times *charisma* (1 Peter 4:10). Still other texts use a Greek word *dorea* (Ephesians 4:7) to speak of the gifts from Christ. Some scholars make a fine distinction between those gifts given to us by God our Creator at our birth, those given to us by Christ to the church, and those given with the infilling of the Holy Spirit. For the purposes of building up servants for the work of ministry in a Church Full of Leaders, we will look at spiritual gifts broadly.

Spiritual Gifts are:

- The tools and endowments given to us by God for doing the work of ministry and fulfilling purpose
- The Spirit-given abilities appropriated for Christian service
- The channels by which the Holy Spirit ministers through the believer
- The building blocks of the church, which are for the perfecting of the saints
- Supernatural capacities, desires, and motivators for service

Spiritual Gifts are not:

- Personality traits
- Means for competing against each other
- Self-serving or glorifying

Spiritual Gifts and the Ministry

God equips believers with the gifts necessary to serve and to lead. Spiritual gifts are the special abilities given to believers in order to minister to and serve the body of Christ. As you help members explore their own giftedness and come to humbly embrace their gifts, they come to accept the unique way in which God has gifted, formed, and equipped them. Members must learn that part of their calling to salvation includes a calling to serve. God is so committed to our serving His church that He has equipped and endowed us especially to serve. Any member not serving is not living up to the purpose and function God intended. We were created in Christ Jesus to serve or walk in good works (Ephesians 2:10).

Once a believer learns how he or she has been gifted, his or her ministry or serving can take on new dimensions of spirituality, authenticity, and confidence. It is encouraging and life giving for believers to know that God has given each a set of spiritual gifts that uniquely mark them for service to God. It is also helpful

for them to know that no gift is more important than another; no gift is less important than another. God gives to each the set of spiritual endowments each will need to serve out his or her purpose and his or her church is one venue for living out his her purpose.

Too often we use the "warm body" method of volunteerism and service. We identify warm bodies in the congregation to serve in a place where we have a need, but they have no passion, no training, and no gifting for the work. However, out of their obedience to pastors, they agree to serve. Clearly, our greatest motivator for service must be love, but too often our love is challenged and diminished when we serve in roles that we are clearly not spiritually equipped or prepared for. Our aim in a Church Full of Leaders is to help people live out their God-given purpose and passion while aligning with other gifted believers to do the work of ministry, fulfill the purposes of the church, and expand the kingdom of God. In this way we each bring what God has given us in service to the body of Christ. No one person or small group can fulfill the totality of the work of ministry, and God has a process by which we each find our place. And when they are in their place serving with gladness (Psalm 100:2), they are engaged in and contributing to the leadership processes of a Church Full of Leaders!

The following Scriptures shed light on the role of spiritual gifts in ministry. Prayerfully read and reflect on these passages:

Romans 12:3-8, NKJV

For I say, through the grace given to me, to everyone who is among you, not to think of himself more highly than he ought to think, but to think soberly, as God has dealt to each one a measure of faith. For as we have many members in one body, but all the members do not have the same function, so we, being many, are one body in Christ, and individually members of one another. Having then gifts differing according to the grace that is given to us, let us use them: if prophecy, let us prophesy in proportion to our faith; or ministry, let us use it in our ministering; he who teaches, in teaching; he who exhorts, in exhortation; he who gives, with liberality; he who leads, with diligence; he who shows mercy, with cheerfulness.

- Serving through spiritual gifting helps keep us humble, reminding us that the gift is operational through the grace of God and not our own initiative, power, or personality.
- We activate, use, and even grow in our gifting by faith.
- Members in the church have different gifting, all of which are necessary and each of which we are expected to use—to God's glory!

1 Corinthians 12:1-31

Now concerning spiritual gifts, brethren, I would not have you ignorant. (vs 1)

- Spiritual gifts were so important to the New Testament church that the

apostle Paul thought it imperative to clarify misconceptions, misuses, and misunderstandings about spiritual gifts.

Now there are diversities of gifts, but the same Spirit. And there are differences of administrations, but the same Lord. And there are diversities of operations, but it is the same God which worketh all in all. (vs 4-6)

- Understanding, embracing, and serving through spiritual gifts honor the diversity God designed into the body of Christ, while at the same time honoring the unity (not uniformity) that comes from the Giver of the gifts.
- Spiritual gifts are not intended to divide the body but to unify us in our distinctives. Even though two believers may have the same spiritual gift, that gift will manifest differently in each person's service as the gift is operated through the unique matrix of human personality, experiences, and context.

But the manifestation of the Spirit is given to every man to profit withal. (vs 7)

- Operating and serving through our spiritual gifts is evidence of the Holy Spirit working through us and is intended for the "profit" or benefit of the body, not just the individual.

But covet earnestly the best gifts: and yet shew I unto you a more excellent way. (vs 31)

- After marvelously enumerating a set of spiritual gifts (there are similar lists given in other passages), using the natural body and its members to illustrate how the spiritual body of Christ works through gifts, Paul reminds the Corinthians and us, that we may try to privilege what we think are the "best" gifts, but in reality, the more excellent way of love supersedes every gift. Thus, we are reminded not to get puffed up in our gifts but to remain humbled to know we are gifted by God and serve through God's love flowing through us.

Ephesians 4:11-12, NKJV
And He Himself gave some to be apostles, some prophets, some evangelists, and some pastors and teachers, for the equipping of the saints for the work of ministry, for the edifying of the body of Christ.

- Some gifts are offices! The office or ministry role itself is the gift to the body of Christ, the church.

- Leadership roles are in and of themselves gifts from God and those who fill such roles do so by the grace of God. People who serve in formal leadership roles are not more significant than other members of the body, but they do provide a critical function for the body of Christ—equipping other members to serve in their "rightful" places.

1 Peter 4:9-11, NKJV

Be hospitable to one another without grumbling. As each one has received a gift, minister it to one another, as good stewards of the manifold grace of God. If anyone speaks, let him speak as the oracles of God. If anyone ministers, let him do it as with the ability which God supplies, that in all things God may be glorified through Jesus Christ, to whom belong the glory and the dominion forever and ever. Amen.

- Spiritual gifts are special graces extended by God and are designed for us to serve one another as good stewards of God's manifold grace.

It is sometimes helpful for people to take a spiritual gifts inventory in which they answer a set of questions related to all the gifts. Taking a spiritual gifts inventory is only one step for believers to discover their spiritual gifts. No inventory can tell believers what their gifts are; they only give clues as to proclivities in ministry areas. Believers discover their gifts through prayer, practice, and patience.

Placing Members into Service

God can and will use a believer wherever He sees fit. However, there are certain gifts that seem particularly well matched to the specific transformative ministries in a Church Full of Leaders. As members prayerfully discover their spiritual gift(s), use that insight to help them discern into which transformative ministry area(s) they might be placed to serve. Placement into a ministry area should never be seen as rigid and lock-stepped but as a dynamic process in which they discern the appropriate place from which to serve at a given time. Encourage members to pray, seek God for clarity, and move forth in faith.

Evangelism Ministries
Evangelism, Prophecy, Teaching, Discernment

Worship Ministries
All

Discipleship and Education Ministries
Teaching, Exhortation, Knowledge, Pastoring/Shepherding

Ministry Development
Administration, Pastoring/Shepherding, Teaching, Exhortation

Connecting Ministries
All, but especially Leadership, Wisdom, Helps, Teaching, Exhortation, Giving, Hospitality

Service Support Ministries
All, but particularly Giving, Serving

Care Ministries
Mercy, Wisdom, Healing

Service/Administration and Operations
Administration, Helps, Leadership

There are leadership and administrative components to each ministry; consequently, there is a place in each ministry for people gifted in administration and/or leadership. There is also a place in every ministry for people with the gift of helps, as they are particularly gifted in finding ways to assist and provide help to others.

As members of your congregation begin to discover their spiritual gifts, some people will find they are serving in areas they are not particularly gifted in. When that occurs, don't make drastic changes to move them to the detriment of the stability of your ministry, but do engage in a process of prayerfully helping people to get in place. Also remind members that believers are often gifted in multiple ways and they may be serving in a place that is not their most pronounced gift but is a part of their overall gift-mix. Finally, we serve in ministry through a combination of gifts and natural skills and ability. Our aim in a Church Full of Leaders is to serve in such a way and in placement such that we bring the best of who we are in terms of skills and gifts to our service and working with others.

Here's the bottom line: there's a place for every member of the body of Christ to serve. And every member of the body of Christ serves a function. As we serve according to our giftedness, according to the spiritual capabilities and endowments given to us by God, we increasingly become a "supporting ligament"; and serving with other gifted people, we truly become "fitly joined together." As each one does its part, the body grows in love (Ephesians 4:16). That is the image of a spiritually gifted community of love; that is the picture of a church full of serving, loving members fully participating with and in the leadership of the church.

Identifying Skills and Abilities for Ministry

Another key dimension for engaging members into ministry is to develop a systematic means for taking inventory of the skills and experiences that exist within your congregation. As is the case with many of the process for churches, there are resources and computer programs for collecting and storing such data. Before your church invests in these programs, you need a systematic process for gathering this information. The Transformative Ministry Matrix provides a framework to think about, pray about, and lay out the skill sets that will be most useful to ministry in your church.

Using the Transformative Ministry Matrix in Chapter 4, you can map out the skills and competencies that will be needed in each ministry area. These skills and competencies can then be used to develop ministry position descriptions for each ministry within the matrix. Remember, in smaller congregations, the functions of the church are led by lay leaders and members and not full-time staff people, as in larger churches with more complex structure and resourcing. Using a systematic approach to identifying members' skills and giftings helps smaller churches remain vibrant and healthy, and the system of engagement serves as a building block for a Church Full of Leaders.

Evangelism & Outreach Ministries

- *Cross-cultural competence*: delivering ministry and messaging that is culturally relevant
- *Organizing teams*: the ability to assemble and assign a team of leaders according to giftings and strengths
- *Oral communication*: the ability communicate the mission and vision of church and ministry programs in both programmatic and meeting settings, inside and outside the church
- *Written communication*: the ability to write clear, concise messages to team members, the congregation, and the community outside the walls of the church that convey the mission and vision of the church
- *Justice advocacy*: the ability to advocate for disenfranchised groups within the community

Worship Ministries

- *Leading worship*: ability to lead and run a worship service from beginning to end, maintaining the sacredness of the time and environment
- *Leading choirs, ensembles*: the ability to organize, teach, and lead music ministry groups
- *Singing*: the ability to deliver the gospel message in song
- *Choreography*: the ability to choreograph liturgical dance numbers that minister the primary message of the church
- *Dance*: the ability to deliver the gospel through movement

- *Musical instruments:* the ability to play an instrument in support of the music ministry of the church, accompanying choirs and soloists
- *Service operations:* oversight of the activities necessary to run a worship service

Discipleship & Education Ministries

- *Teaching adults:* trained to develop and teach Christian education courses to adults *Teaching teens:* trained to adapt Sunday school lessons for a teen audience
- *Teaching children:* training to adapt Sunday school lessons for children
- *Instructional design:* the ability to develop Christian education courses outside the International Sunday school curriculum
- *Education administration:* the ability to oversee the ongoing development and delivery of the church's education ministry, including classes and teachers
- *Arts and crafts:* the ability to develop and implement creative projects into classroom learning, particularly for children and/or teens

Ministry Development

- *Leadership development:* developing and implementing ongoing trainings or conferences for those who serve in ministry
- *Ministerial training and development:* the ability to organize and train local church ministers
- *Planning:* developing plans to carry out ministry programming, activities, etc.
- *Facilitation:* the ability to facilitate workshops, etc.
- *Data and survey design and analysis:* the ability to design and analyze surveys used for the ongoing development of ministry
- *Change management:* the ability to communicate and implement change to ministry team members, the congregation, and/or community without major disruption or upheaval

Connecting & Fellowship Ministries

- *Program design and development:* the ability to design programming that is tailored to the needs of the church's demographics
- *Logistical skills:* ability to attend to the details of ministry operations
- *Marketing:* strong communication, public relations skills to help market the church overall and specific programming, to manage the messaging of the church
- *Budgeting:* developing and managing financial plans for executing ministry
- *Meeting facilitation:* planning and running effective ministry meetings

Care Ministries

- *Care for the poor:* sensitivity and understanding in serving/meeting needs of members or community members with financial challenges
- *Care for the elderly:* understanding and attending to the needs of the senior population
- *Crisis care:* meeting emergency needs (e.g., counseling, home visits, hospital visits)
- *Equipping others for care giving:* training others to serve in pastoral care and personal service ministry areas such as support groups, funeral/ homegoing, career ministry
- *Hospital visitations:* visiting ill members or relatives of members to offer prayer, represent pastoral staff

Administrative Ministries

- *Accounting:* demonstrating an acumen of accounting principles
- *Marketing communication:* developing and delivering creative messages that convey the mission, vision, and programs of the church
- *IT:* oversight of church's computer system
- *Digital media:* oversight of church's social media platforms
- *Graphic design:* creation of print and electronic forms of marketing (e.g., brochure, Web site)
- *Leading stewardship processes:* oversight of recruitment ministry

Operations Ministries

- *Food services:* oversight of food services, including preparing and serving food for ministry programs, special events
- *Maintenance:* upkeep of church facilities, interior and exterior
- *Landscaping:* maintenance of plants, shrubs, and related visual elements that decorate church grounds
- *Audio/Visual:* set-up of audio/visual (sound, video) for worship services, classroom instruction, ministry programs, etc.
- *Media production:* production and editing of video for ministry delivered via Web, television, etc.
- *Editing:* proofreading of print materials to ensure accuracy of messaging
- *Hospitality:* greeting members and visitors as they enter the church building
- *Member services:* fulfilling requests for tithing envelopes, address changes, membership status, etc.

Identifying Future Leaders

Of those seven servants (referred to as deacons) who were chosen to serve the poor in the church, we know of two who would go on to make a significant

impact in the building of God's kingdom. Stephen, who "did great wonders and signs among the people," became the first Christian martyr as he preached the gospel (Acts 7:54-60). After his execution, persecution of Christians increased and they were scattered abroad. As a result, deacons became evangelists or missionaries, due to the need.[6] One of those deacons was Philip, who preached in Samaria and is best known for converting the Ethiopian eunuch (Acts 8:26-40). This demonstrates that we are always growing, even in our service to God and His people; therefore, it is critical that we tap into the leadership potential of those tasked with carrying about the behind-the-scenes work of the church.

Like the apostles, we constantly pray for and seek to develop the leadership potential in those who serve well after they have been placed and are growing in their service and faith. That becomes easy to do when we nurture relationships with them that go beyond serving alongside them. They are relationships of accountability that not only help believers mature in their faith and realize their full potential as servants and leaders in God's kingdom, but they also help ministries grow. It speaks to the issue of retaining servants once we effectively place them where God has called them to be and making room for new members to serve as they come into the family.

When leaders develop and effectively carry out strategic processes for engaging more believers in ministry, recruitment efforts are more successful, retention is strengthened, and growth is assured, because believers are apt to be properly placed, understand the "big" picture of ministry, and value their role as part-owners of ministry.

Structure Needed:

Ministry Engagement Process (MEP) Team: The MEP team will consist of a ministry team lead and team members charged with coordinating the ministry engagement process.

MEP Team Members will be responsible for
1. Customizing the MEP process provided in this Church Full of Leaders manual to their own church
2. Communicating MEP needs and instructions to members
3. Working with ministry leaders to develop a ministry engagement booklet and forms and provide instructions as needed
4. Following up on completed MEP forms
5. Interviewing members interested in new service assignments
6. Tracking member serving process (a basic spreadsheet may suffice initially, but as the church grows there are applications and software that can help)
7. Providing status reports to pastoral leaders

Tools Needed:

Ministry Opportunity Booklet–a list and description of the ministry opportunities that are available for members to serve in. The ministry engagement leader works with the leaders of each ministry to list the ministry, its purpose statement, and the various places in each ministry where interested members can serve. Any special requirements for serving in the ministry would be listed here as well (e.g., to serve in youth ministry, all members have to complete a background check and attend a youth safety training). The booklet or handout must be updated regularly.

Ministry Engagement Forms–A form for members to complete that gives their demographic and contact information; provides space for them to share their skills, talents, spiritual gifts, educational background and ministry/work/volunteer experiences; and space for them to declare the ministry areas they are interested in or want more information about. See Appendix G for a sample.

Process needed:

1. Current and new members need to be taught the biblical significance of offering their gifts and talents by serving in ministry, as well as be kept informed of the places and opportunities to serve with other believers. Regular communication of the needs of ministry will be important, whether through Sunday bulletin announcements or inserts, blurbs in the Sunday morning video/PowerPoint announcements or the church's Web site.
2. Keep the Ministry Engagement Forms handy, so members can pick one up (e.g., in the church office or at a place designated as the MEP kiosk or station) or download from the Web site. Make sure the instructions for submitting the completed form are simple and clear. Make sure someone from the MEP gathers, reviews, and follows up with interested members promptly.
3. Interview process. The MEP will serve as the first point of contact to have conversation with members interested in serving and will submit their contact info to the leaders of the appropriate ministry, or set up a meeting for the member and ministry leader to talk.
4. Ministry leaders should make sure members to their ministries receive proper orientation to the ministry.
5. The MEP will follow up with ministry leaders to ensure members have been properly placed and their serving experience is going well.

Chapter 8—Reflection

1. Does the Pareto Principle (the 80-20 rule) impact your current servanthood base? If so, why do you think that is so?

2. What current methods do you use to draw members who have never served before? Which do you find to be the most effective?

3. Currently, how do you determine whether or not a new servant is the "right" fit for the ministry with which he or she is seeking to serve? How do you help those who serve discover their spiritual gifts?

Many churches are started by entrepreneurial leaders who are innovative and charismatic. They attract others to the ministry based on their God-given gifts. The culture of these new churches often reflects the style of the leader. As more people are drawn to the church, the pastor needs to engage more leaders to do the work of ministry. It is critical as more leaders are engaged that the way of doing ministry at a particular church is codified so that others can follow. This codification of the way we do ministry is known as process.

As the church grows around a dynamic teaching and preaching ministry, the development of administrative processes is critical. Sometimes leaders like doing the "work of ministry" (e.g., feeding the homeless, teaching Bible studies, leading small groups) but dislike attending to other administrative tasks (e.g., filling out forms, tracking expenses, and managing budgets). Every wise leader at every level of the church understands that administration of ministry is critical to the church. In chapter 5, we looked at the five transformative processes of ministry—evangelism, worship, education, fellowship, and service. They are the broad, purposeful areas of ministry by which the purposes of transformation are achieved. For each of the broad areas of ministry, specific processes for getting things done must be established.

The Ministry of Administration

Too often administration is not seen as "real" ministry. In some circles, administration is seen as secondary to preaching and pastoral care ministries. In response to its rapid growth and the complexity of needs that manifested in a culturally diverse congregation, the leaders of the early New Testament church prayerfully sought leaders to oversee the daily practical affairs of the church, such as the task of distributing food to the widows of the congregation.

These leaders had to be of good reputation and full of the Holy Spirit and wisdom; to them was appointed the "business" of the church (Acts 6:3), leaving the apostles to focus on prayer and preaching. Likewise today, church growth demands organizing ministry functions according to the needs of the congregation.

The term administration is found in Scriptures to describe ministry functions related to serving to the organizational and practical needs of the church, in support of the spiritual needs of the church. Stemming from the Greek word *diakonia,* administration means to administer or serve in specific offices. Broadly, *diakonia* could stand for the office of the apostle (prophet, evangelist, elder, etc.) and its administration. Or it could stand more specifically for the ministration of those who help meet needs by collecting or distributing charities. *Diakonia* also stood for the office of the deacon or those who rendered service to help the church.

Five Elements of Effective Administration of Ministry

Purpose–the reason for which something exists; the reason something is done or created (Ephesians 1:5-13). Every activity of ministry must have a purpose that aligns with the broad transformative purpose of the church. Too often we hear people in churches talk about an activity that they've done for years, but no one can recall why they are still doing it. Process is always in service to purpose. Administrative processes help us achieve the purposes of ministry.

Passion–Just as process serves purpose, passion is the energy that fuels ministry purpose (1 Thessalonians 2:13; Philippians 2:13; Colossians 1:29). So administrative processes don't become rigid, rote activities that bind people, these administrative procedures must be clear yet flexible enough to allow leaders to minster from their passion.

Process–is a systematic series of actions directed to some end. A process defines "what" needs to be done and which roles are involved. Administrative processes provide a plan for ministry that enables us to achieve consistent, repeatable results (Proverbs 20:18; Jeremiah 29:11), an ability to manage resources, and maintain accountability in ministry.

People–at the heart of ministry purpose are the people we serve and with whom we serve (Ephesians 4:11-12). Administrative processes are put in place to allow leaders to get ministry accomplished through people. People who serve in ministry must understand the administrative and programmatic procedures necessary to develop programs that meet the needs of ministry members, communicate ministry goals, request and track ministry funds, and ascertain needs of ministry members.

Pursuit of Excellence–the quality standard to which we strive in fulfilling ministry purpose (Philippians 1:9-11) and by which we structure our processes and procedures. Administrative processes that are clear, not overly rigid, and easily communicated help ministry leaders pursue excellence.

Each church must develop or secure a set of administrative processes that facilitate communication among ministry leaders, protect resources. In a Church Full of Leaders, leaders of various ministries can come together to map out the church's current processes and develop forms and instructions that codify these processes. Following is a list of processes your church should have in place.

Basic Ministry Processes for Ministry and Auxiliary Leaders

Following are a list of ministry processes that can be led by a combination of volunteer and paid leaders. The ministry teams responsible for each administrative process can develop protocols and operating guidelines for leaders to follow. The leader of administration will want to collect all procedures and accompanying forms into a manual of standard administrative and operational procedures for all leaders. This manual should be accessible to all leaders. There are a variety of cost effective (or free) apps and programs that can be used to automate these processes. As your church continues to grow, the systems will need to be integrated for proper reporting and tracking.

- New Member Intake
- Member Communication
    - Change of Address
    - Giving Statements
- Program Development and Approval
- Ministry Engagement (Servant Placement, Development, and Management)
- Program/Event Management Process
    - Event Request
    - Request for Sunday Announcement
    - Request for Posting Announcement to Web site and Social Media
    - Event feedback
- Ministry/Auxiliary Financial Process
    - Budget Template
    - Dues/Event Collections
    - Purchase Order Request
    - Check Request
    - Expense Reimbursement
- Emergency and Safety Procedures

Note: accounting and general church financial processes are not included, as these are typically handled by paid staff or contract accountants/bookkeepers.

Reflect on the clarity of your ministry processes in each of the following areas. On a scale from 1 (low) to 10 (high), rate how clear each process is for ministry leaders and/or ministers to follow, rate how effective each process is, and note whether or not there is an online/computerized template or a hard copy form for each process.

	Clear	Effective	Computerized Form/ Procedure	Hard Copy Form/Procedure
Membership Communication				
New Member Intake				
Member Giving Statement				
Member Change of Address				
Program Development & Approval (for program leaders)				
Speaker Request/ Approval				
Event Management				
Space/Resource Request				
Request for Sunday Announcement				
Request for Web site/Social Media/ E-Blast Program, PR				
Volunteer Recruiting & Development				
Ministry Financial Processes				
Program Budget Template				
Purchase Order Request				
Check Request				
Expense Reimbursement & Report				
Emergency & Safety Procedure				
Others				

Chapter 9–Reflection

Administrative Process Analysis

1. What processes need to be clarified?

2. What processes need to be communicated more broadly to all leaders?

3. What processes need to be communicated more broadly to the membership?

4. What forms need to be updated and/or automated?

5. If not already in place, what computer application/software might our church secure to facilitate our core processes? If already in place, which of our software/application programs need to be upgraded and/or updated?

Just as God formed the first human out of the dust of the ground, God is forming us into the likeness of Christ. It's a spiritual formation, or a transformation of heart, mind, and soul. The apostle Paul declared to the churches of Galatia that he prayed continually for them, actually travailing as a woman giving birth, until Christ would be formed in them. (Galatians 4:19)

The forming or formation of which Paul spoke stems from the Greek word morpho. It speaks of a molding or a full development. Paul's hope for the believers in Galatia specifically, and all believers generally, was that the character of Christ would become fully developed in them. This development is a process of spiritual growth and maturity in Christ that changes the believer on many levels. Thus, to be transformed (meta-morphoo) is to be formed on many levels, and ultimately at a deep level of believing and thinking that manifests externally in behaving and living. Like a stream, or an energy current, through every dimension of the believer's life, flows the transforming power of the Holy Spirit—the ultimate transformer.

Please know that spiritual transformation is not an event that can be accomplished in a conference or training class. Spiritual transformation is an ongoing process of growth, development, and maturity. A Church Full of Leaders needs spiritually mature leaders that help to facilitate the spiritual growth processes of the church. It needs leaders who are sensitive to the transforming work of God, such that God beckons us into deeper relationship with Him and in so doing moves us from self-centeredness, to more Christ-centeredness; from the trappings of false identity of roles, to our true identities in Christ; from a life of people pleasing and over-functioning, to a life of purpose and focus.

There are many books, resources, and retreat centers that can help a church with its spiritual formation processes. The aim of this section is to get you started in thinking about the ongoing transformation of the leaders of your church. Here we will concentrate on that vertical relationship—that between the Lord and us—and how our personal attention to it, through spiritual disciplines, makes all the difference in our horizontal relationships—that between us and others, particularly those whom we serve and serve alongside.

Transformation may be likened unto a journey—the movement or passing from one state or level of spirituality to another, more mature level. That state or level of maturity is sometimes referred to as a "place in God," and it really is referring to a leader's depth of relationship with the Lord that is manifest or evidenced by her relationships with and service to others. Transformation occurs deep within our hearts, as our mind-sets are changed and emanate into a different set of behaviors, more mature relationships, and life. Transformation can be said to be an inner work yielding outer results.

Leaders must never forget that the work of transforming hearts is a work of God through the lordship of Jesus Christ and the indwelling power of the Holy Spirit. God is gracious to enlist us into the process by creating us to walk in good works (Ephesians 2:8-10). Church leadership is one such vehicle.

Church leadership at its heart is a spiritual endeavor, and pastoral teams and church leadership developers must intentionally attend to the processes that help to form spiritually mature leaders—including themselves. Though a Church Full of Leaders is ultimately about engaging and mobilizing more of the congregation into service and the processes of transformation, each of us comes to leadership from varying levels of relationship with the Lord.

How leaders work with congregants and how they speak to other leaders all flow from the very heart of the leader. Whether it's a small group we lead or a complex ministry organization, every leader must remember he or she leads from within. Motives for leading, attitudes toward those we lead and serve, and dispositions toward other leaders start in the heart of the leader. And as the leader surrenders to the work of the Holy Spirit in his or her heart, the leader remains open to the move of the Spirit to form and transform him or her into the man or woman God intends for him or her to become.

God uses a myriad of things to transform us. He even uses our leadership assignments to help conform us into the image of Jesus (Romans 8:29). Working and serving with brothers and sisters of varying backgrounds and experiences can be fraught with challenges and take leaders through changes. How leaders handle these challenges and changes will reveal their level of spiritual maturity.

As much as we focus on building the skills of the leader, we must likewise help to cultivate the heart of the leader for God and for others. There are a number of approaches to spiritual formation for leaders, as well as tools and experiences that help the leader take time to attend to his or her spirituality.

Spiritual formation for leaders is a lifelong journey, not an event. Conferences and training sessions are great, but in a Church Full of Leaders, leaders must be encouraged to reflect on their relationships and must make space to respond to the Spirit's promptings and urgings. Practicing daily disciplines of prayer, Bible reading, and worship are essential for leaders. Developing regular rhythms of Sabbath keeping, solitude, and fasting are essential for leaders. Spiritual practices that do not become routine and hackneyed, but facilitate the upward journey toward God, the journey within, and the outward journey to serve, are essential for leaders.

Following is a broad-based approach that you will want to consider as you help your leaders to grow spiritually.

Always start with God. Know that God is the Sovereign Lord of your life. The journey is aimed at bringing us closer to the Lord and bringing us more and more into surrender to His lordship.

> We are citizens of God's kingdom—the kingdom of heaven. And we live by the principles of the kingdom. Jesus as God's King comes to rule in our hearts, and when Jesus is truly on the throne of our hearts—there are certain things that manifest in our lives and in our character. The journey becomes about walking worthy of the vocation wherewith we have been called (Ephesians 4:1), and it becomes about pleasing the King.

Understand the nature and context of the journey. We live or exist at two levels—the natural/earthly and the spiritual/heavenly.

> The earthly dimension consists of the world system and the values of this world. As believers and Christian leaders, we are "in the world but not of it." We are called as salt and light to be transforming agents in the world. The spiritual dimension consists of the invisible world, the kingdom of God that is already but not yet. According to Colossians 1:13-14, Jesus delivered us from the power of darkness and conveyed or translated us into the kingdom of the Son of His love, in whom we have redemption through His blood, the forgiveness of sins. According to Ephesians 2:1, 5, "You he made alive who were dead in trespasses and sins; He made us alive together with Christ…and raised us up together, and made us sit together in the heavenly places in Christ Jesus" and Colossians 3:1-2, "if then you were raised with Christ, seek those things which are above where Christ is sitting at the right hand of God. Set your mind on things above, not on things of the earth."

Build Leader's Identity in Christ

In Christ, the believer has been translated into His kingdom—the realm of God's sovereign rule and reign. In Christ we are blessed, adopted, chosen, and accepted (Ephesians 1:3-6).

In fact, according to Scripture, because we are in Christ, we are:

- The righteousness of God in Christ Jesus (2 Corinthians 5:21)
- More than conquerors through Him who loved us (Romans 8:37)
- Accepted in the Beloved (Ephesians 1:6)
- Children of God (John 1:12,13)
- Members of Christ's body (1 Corinthians 12:27)
- Complete in Christ (Colossians 2: 9,10)
- Born of God, and the evil one cannot touch us (1 John 5:18-20)

Every believer must really know his or her identity in Christ, especially leaders. Our identity shapes our behavior and choices. The most effective leaders lead from a place of clear identity in and identification with Christ!

Help Leaders to Understand the Will of God. Leaders in our congregations have to discern the will of God and understand what it means to yield to the Lord's will and not be solely driven by their own will. Leadership is about aligning our will to God's will.

As we are reminded in Colossians 1:9-12, leaders especially must pray to "be filled with the knowledge of God's will in all wisdom and spiritual understanding." We must pray that we walk worthy of the Lord and that we truly please the Lord in our leadership. And we must pray that our leadership is "fruitful in every good work." Clearly none of this can happen unless we are "strengthened with all might according to God's glorious power working in us.

The ability to discern God's will is critical to effectively delivering ministry and leading others who serve. Leaders must be taught how and reminded to seek God's direction for shaping and delivering ministry, as well as leading others.

Encourage leaders to align their words with the Word of God. What comes out of a leader's mouth helps to shape his or her destiny and that of the ministry or organization he or she leads. The leader's words affect the people she or he leads. Leaders who murmur and complain create dissonance within their teams and ministries and hinder the progress of their ministries. Leaders who compliment, praise, and affirm create an empowering atmosphere that honors God and builds up their people. These are not merely psychological principles; they are spiritual principles. God instructed Moses to send twelve spies to go into the new land that had been promised to them to scope it out and bring back a report. Ten spies came back with a bad report saying, "We are not able to go up against the people" (Numbers 13:31). Their words did not line up with what God had said. God said He was giving them the land. Then their report should have been that of Caleb, "We are well able to overcome it" (Numbers 13:30b). Unfortunately, the words of the majority rippled through the congregation, incited fear among

the people, and created a world of unbelief and doubt. They were hampered and could not move forward.

Finally, we cannot program transformation as we do an educational curriculum. Transformation does not come about by neatly checking boxes of a spiritual practices to-do list, or methodically following a spiritual growth plan. According to Ruth Haley Barton, author of *Sacred Rhythms*:

> *Even though it is normal for each and every redeemed person to experience spiritual transformation, something about it will always remain a mystery to us. It is one thing to be able to tweak and control external behaviors; it is another thing to experience those internal seismic shifts that change the way I exist in this world.*[1]

She goes on to say,

> *In the end, this is the most hopeful thing any of us can say about spiritual transformation: I cannot transform myself, or anyone else for that matter. What I can do is create the conditions in which spiritual transformation can take place, by developing and maintaining a rhythm of spiritual practices that keep me open and available to God.*[2]

Chapter 10—Reflection

1. Our identity shapes our behavior and choices. What most informs your identity—how you view yourself and define yourself as a leader?

2. The ability to discern God's will is critical to effectively delivering ministry and leading others who serve. In what ways do you seek God's direction for how to shape and deliver ministry, as well as lead others?

3. The Word of God is essential for transforming the mind of the leader. How has your personal Bible study strengthened your leadership?

4. Worship—private and corporate—draws us closer to God. As a leader, do you incorporate worship in your team meetings? For example, does your ministry group sing a praise song or hymn, read a Scripture before commencing a meeting? If so, in what way has it impacted ministry delivery?

Leaders are fast paced, often busy people who (sometimes mistakenly) pride ourselves in running things, being in charge, and keeping things going. What we forget is that, even as leaders, we are first and foremost called into relationship with our heavenly Father through the redemptive work of Jesus Christ. Our Christian lives and leadership are journeys in which we walk with the Lord; our relationship with the Lord sustains us and moves us to our ultimate destiny. Because we are prone to doing instead of being, a crucial part of leadership formation is to take time to reflect on our spiritual walk—the outgrowth of our being with the Lord.

There are eight dimensions of the spiritual walk explored in the Spiritual Walk Inventory (SWI) for Ministry Leaders. Following are instructions for taking the brief 40-item questionnaire.

The Spiritual Walk Inventory ™ for Ministry Leaders

A Christian's "walk" has often been used to refer to the general state of the Christian's spiritual life. The depth and direction of the Christian leader's "walk" has bearing on his or her ability to set the spiritual tone for his or her ministry. The Spiritual Walk Inventory™ (SWI) is designed to help you assess and reflect on your spiritual walk and, thus, your spiritual leadership.

Rate yourself on various dimensions of the spiritual walk in the 40 statements that follow. Circle only one number per statement. Your first response to a statement is typically the most accurate response, so don't spend too much time overanalyzing any one statement. The questionnaire is for your use only, so please be as honest as possible when responding. You will gain the most insight from the SWI when you respond as you truly believe you currently are, and not as you wish you were, in the way you feel you should be, in the way you think others feel you are, or in the way that was true for you at some other time.

Use the following scale to circle the response that most closely describes how true each statement is for you. If the statement does not apply to you, circle 0.

Does Not Apply	0
Not at All True	1
A Little True	2
Somewhat True	3
Considerably True	4
Totally True	5

1. I trust God to provide me with insight, direction, and guidance in addressing issues.	0 1 2 3 4 5
2. I face challenges with an optimistic attitude and an expectation that God will work out situations for good.	0 1 2 3 4 5
3. I rely upon the promises found in God's Word to endure difficulty.	0 1 2 3 4 5
4. I regularly pray and confess God's Word to achieve success.	0 1 2 3 4 5
5. I maintain hope in God for the future, although outcomes are not readily evident.	0 1 2 3 4 5
6. I daily spend time in prayer, worship, and devotional reading in order to be more sensitive to the presence and voice of God.	0 1 2 3 4 5
7. I attend, participate, and/or engage in regular Bible study in order to more accurately discern the will and mind of God.	0 1 2 3 4 5
8. I seek the guidance of the Holy Spirit to discern options and correct paths for my life and leadership.	0 1 2 3 4 5
9. I repent and forgive more readily in order to keep my heart uncluttered and open to the voice of the Spirit.	0 1 2 3 4 5
10. I am careful with what I read and watch so as not to dull my sensitivity to the Spirit.	0 1 2 3 4 5
11. God has a plan for my life and leadership.	0 1 2 3 4 5
12. I have a clear sense of God's purpose for my life.	0 1 2 3 4 5
13. Leading and serving in the church/ministry brings significance and meaning to my life.	0 1 2 3 4 5
14. I am intentional and purposeful in my leadership actions.	0 1 2 3 4 5
15. Knowing God's purpose for my life and leadership helps me focus on what is important.	0 1 2 3 4 5
16. Who I am inside is as important to my leadership as the skills I possess.	0 1 2 3 4 5

17. My attitude reflects that of an maturing Christian leader.	0 1 2 3 4 5
18. I am aware of both my strengths and weaknesses and don't pretend to be perfect.	0 1 2 3 4 5
19. I am honest with myself and those I lead/serve about my beliefs and thoughts.	0 1 2 3 4 5
20. When operating in my leadership role, my actions (what I do) honestly reflect my interior life (how I believe, think, and feel).	0 1 2 3 4 5
21. My motivation for serving is to demonstrate love to others.	0 1 2 3 4 5
22. I remain sensitive to the needs of others without judging them.	0 1 2 3 4 5
23. I give of myself and my substance without expecting anything in return.	0 1 2 3 4 5
24. I willingly make the sacrifices that are required of ministry leaders.	0 1 2 3 4 5
25. I pray to maintain Christ's attitude of kindness and grace toward all of those whom I serve and lead.	0 1 2 3 4 5
26. I spend regular time in fellowship with other believers/ministry leaders for mutual support.	0 1 2 3 4 5
27. I establish and maintain healthy relationships in my church/ministry.	0 1 2 3 4 5
28. I consider it part of my responsibility to safeguard the unity of my church/ministry.	0 1 2 3 4 5
29. My actions and attitude as a leader are important in developing and maintaining a sense of community in my congregation/ministry.	0 1 2 3 4 5
30. I forthrightly confront strife and dysfunctional conflict in the ministry.	0 1 2 3 4 5
31. Christian leadership is as much about moral authority as it is about spiritual authority.	0 1 2 3 4 5
32. I repent and confess sin readily without letting sinful behaviors become a practice.	0 1 2 3 4 5
33. I understand that my spiritual condition impacts the life of the church/ministry I lead.	0 1 2 3 4 5
34. I consider how my choices affect the ministry/church I lead.	0 1 2 3 4 5
35. I choose to refrain from activities that do not nurture my spirit.	0 1 2 3 4 5

36. I daily seek the Lord for making decisions and choices that affect my life and my ministry/congregation.	0 1 2 3 4 5
37. When making decisions, I seek input and perspectives from a group of trusted advisors, confidantes, and/or wise counselors.	0 1 2 3 4 5
38. I have a formal group to whom I remain accountable for my leadership decisions.	0 1 2 3 4 5
39. I learn from my failures and do not get mired in past mistakes.	0 1 2 3 4 5
40. My ability to make wise choices has improved as I have grown in my relationship with the Lord.	0 1 2 3 4 5

Scoring Sheet

Faith	Spiritual Sensitivity	Purpose	Godly Character	Love	Unity	Holiness	Wisdom
Add your scores for questions 1-5 and place this sub-total in the space below	Add your scores for questions 6-10 and place this sub-total in the space below	Add your scores for questions 11-15 and place this sub-total in the space below	Add your scores for questions 16-20 and place this sub-total in the space below	Add your scores for questions 21-25 and place this sub-total in the space below	Add your scores for questions 26-30 and place this sub-total in the space below	Add your scores for questions 31-35 and place this sub-total in the space below	Add your scores for questions 36-40 and place this sub-total in the space below
_____	_____	_____	_____	_____	_____	_____	_____

Qualities of Spiritual Leaders

- **Faith**—demonstrating the ability to trust God in leadership situations and to remain hopeful even in negative circumstances. Faith fuels the ability for leaders to trust God and not to be over-reactive, over-controlling, or over-functioning.
- **Spiritual sensitivity**—demonstrating the ability to be sensitive to or in tune with the Holy Spirit, as well as one's own interior life. This inner sensitivity helps to shape a leader's ability to be sensitive or empathetic to others, and to remain sensitive to ministry, organizational, and team dynamics.
- **Purpose**—expressing and living out a clear reason for being, leading with intentionality. Purpose fuels passion and enables leaders to focus on the higher aims and goals of a ministry or organization.
- **Godly character**—possessing the inner qualities, disposition, and conviction that reflect the "mark" of God on the leader, and are also evident in the leader's choices and attitudes.
- **Love**—demonstrating a motive for leadership that is fueled by the love of Christ and is "other-directed." Leading with love means to show a concern and care for others so that others come to trust your motives. Love-motivated leadership ensures people that a leader is not self-serving and will act in the best interest of the ministry and the people.
- **Unity**—demonstrating the ability to establish and maintain healthy relationships in the organization or ministry, as well as resolving conflict in ways that help to build and maintain community.
- **Holiness**—demonstrating a lifestyle that resonates with biblical principles, living out a set of values that resonant with the fruit of the Spirit and Christian ethical and moral standards.
- **Wisdom**—possessing the capacity to assess situations or circumstances judiciously and to draw sound conclusions.

Faith

We walk by faith and not by sight. ~2 Corinthians 5:7

Leadership is an act of faith. It is an act of faith to speak of a preferred future that is not visible as though it already existed. Whether rallying a team behind a ministry program, inspiring a congregation in a desired direction, or moving a ministry department toward goals and objectives, leaders must demonstrate complete trust and reliance upon God and God's Word to achieve outcomes only known by God.

The ability to trust God is critical to Christian leadership. In fact, without faith, it is impossible to please God (Hebrews 11:6). Doubt, fear, worry, and control are all enemies of healthy Christian leadership. Not only do these things hinder our walk with Christ, but they also hinder our ability to work together with and lead other believers. Spiritual leadership is invigorated by a belief in God that enables the leader to walk victoriously, and face new challenges with optimism empowered by the Holy Spirit and a firm expectation that God will work all things together for our good (Romans 8:28).

Faith is a force within us that leads us to act, often in spite of what appears to be the hopelessness of situations. Fear tells us to give up, we can't take it, and can't go on. Faith assures us that God is on our side and has a plan for our lives. Faith tells us that with God all things are possible (Matthew 19:26). Faith gives us the courage and energy to continue to stand in spite of temporary setbacks or failure. Never forget we are commanded to build [ourselves] up on our most holy faith, praying in the Holy Spirit (Jude 20), suggesting that the inward power of the Holy Spirit invigorates and fuels our faith.

Review statements 1-5 on the SWI and mark those you scored a 4 or 5. Use a different mark to indicate those questions you scored a 1 or 2.

Spiritual Sensitivity

Walk according to the Spirit. ~Romans 8:1-7
Do not walk according to the flesh. ~Romans 8:1
Walk in the Spirit and you shall not fulfill the lust of the flesh. ~Galatians 5:16

The Christian life includes our walking in the Spirit, being sensitive to the things of the Spirit, having our minds set on what the Holy Spirit desires, and having our minds controlled by the Holy Spirit (Romans 8:5-6). As ministry leaders, to walk according to the Spirit is also to live with such spiritual sensitivity as to hear and heed the heart and mind of God for the people and organizations you lead. The work of transformation to which we are dedicated is a work of the Holy Spirit. We as leaders are mere participants in the transforming work of God in the lives of members of our ministry organizations.

Carnality hinders the spiritual walk and your ability to be sensitive to what God wants for your life and your work in ministry. Those who live according to the sinful nature have their minds set on what that nature desires (Romans 8:5); those controlled by the sinful nature cannot please God (Romans 8:8). Cultivating the life in the Spirit is essential and developing and practicing regular, consistent spiritual disciplines (prayer, fasting, reading/studying the Word, meditating, worship, serving, fellowship, journaling, learning, personal devotions) is essential to enhancing and maintaining your spiritual sensitivity.

Review statements 6 - 10 on the SWI and mark those you scored a 4 or 5. Use a different mark to indicate those questions you scored a 1 or 2.

Purpose

Walk worthy of the vocation (calling) wherewith you have been called.
~Ephesians 4:1
For we are his workmanship, created in Christ Jesus for good works, which God prepared beforehand that we should walk in them. ~Ephesians 2:10

God has a purpose for you. He created you on purpose and for a purpose. This purpose is the reason you were born and placed here on the earth at this point in history. Knowing your purpose helps you stay focused. Knowing your purpose provides direction for your life. Knowing your purpose fuels your Christian walk and your spiritual leadership. Understanding purpose is critical to the spiritual walk of every believer but is exponentially important for ministry leaders. God created you on purpose and for a purpose. The clearer you are on that purpose, the more clearly you come to understand what pleases God and how you can please God through your self-development, service, and stewardship.

A Christian who is not clear on purpose tends to walk aimlessly, is unfulfilled and frustrated, and consequently brings a lot of negative energy to the ministry activities of which he or she is a part. Seek to clarify purpose by understanding general principles of the Christian's purpose, as well as by exploring your specific purpose as evidence in spiritual gifts, talents, skills, and experiences. I hope you can truly say that what you do in service/ministry is part of your calling and purpose. What you do is essential to the community and to the kingdom.

Review statements 11-15 on the SWI and mark those you scored a 4 or 5. Use a different mark to indicate those questions you scored a 1 or 2.

Godly Character

Walk humbly with your God. ~Micah 6:8
Walk as children of Light. ~Isaiah 50:11
I have no greater joy than to hear that my children walk in truth. ~1 John 4
Let us walk properly (decently). ~Romans 13:13

The above Scriptures refer to some dimensions of character: humility, integrity, and honesty. Character development is a primary aim of the Christian walk, and godly character is essential for ministry leaders.

Character is the sum total of who you are. It comprises your mental, emotional, spiritual, and cognitive qualities. Your character is the core part of you—the real you—and it affects the choices you make, the lifestyle you take, the promises you make, and your ability to lead with integrity. For Christians in general and ministry leaders specifically, godly character is the marked expression of God upon a person's life. The evident stamp of God upon a person's inner being and reflected in his or her outer actions.

Cultivating the qualities of the inner life, attitude, and inner perspective are essential to a healthy outer walk. Becoming self-aware, understanding and accepting your own patterns of thoughts, feelings, desires, dreams, motivations, and triggers, is essential to healthy ministry leadership.

Review statements 16-20 on the SWI and mark those you scored a 4 or 5. Use a different mark to indicate those questions you scored a 1 or 2.

Love

Walk in love as Christ also has loved us and given himself for us. ~Ephesians 5:1

As ministry leaders, the ultimate motivation for anything we do must be love. It cannot be to please people, to gain a title, pat on the back, or accolades from others. Without love, even our most gracious, charitable acts are meaningless (1 Corinthians 13:3), and without love our gifts are rendered in vain (1 Corinthians 13:2). We cannot truly lead as God intended, and we cannot serve others without an attitude and motivation of love. Lack of love, insensitivity to the needs of others, and callousness toward the feelings of others suggests both spiritual immaturity and deep hurts that cause ministry members to hurt others.

To have an attitude of love is to take on Christ's perspective of kindness, grace, and unconditional love for others.

Review statements 21-25 on the SWI and mark those you scored a 4 or 5. Use a different mark to indicate those questions you scored a 1 or 2.

Unity

Let us walk by the same rule, let us be of the same mind. ~Philippians 3:16

The ability to establish and maintain healthy relationships and the capacity to build community are marks of a healthy spiritual walk and healthy ministry leadership. We do not walk this spiritual journey by ourselves; God placed us in the fellowship of believers to aid, enhance, and support our mutual walk. Ministry leaders cultivate unity through their behaviors, their decisions, and

their attitudes. Ministry leaders also can destroy unity through their behaviors, decisions, and attitudes.

Discord, dissension, and unresolved conflict diminish our ability to work and serve together. Can two walk together unless they are agreed (Amos 3:3)? You cannot walk or effectively work in a ministry with unresolved conflicts. Neither can ministry members walk or work together without a means for handling conflicts and disagreements that will inevitably arise. Times of refreshing, retreats are necessary for building the relational unity that God calls us to. Our ministries are not all work, not all task oriented.

Review statements 26-30 on the SWI and mark those you scored a 4 or 5. Use a different mark to indicate those questions you scored a 1 or 2.

Holiness

Just as you received from us how you ought to walk and to please God. ~1 Thessalonians 4:1
So that he may establish your hearts blameless in holiness before our God at the coming of our Lord Jesus Christ with all the saints. ~1 Thessalonians 3:13
For this is the will of God, your sanctification: that you should abstain from sexual immorality, that each of you should know how to possess his own vessel in sanctification and honor, not in passion of lust, like the Gentiles, who do not know God; that no one should take advantage of and defraud his brother in this matter...For God did not call us to uncleanness, but in holiness.
~1 Thessalonians 4:3-7

Christian leaders represent Christ and are charged with living an exemplary life of holiness. Christian leaders are not perfect but are being perfected (matured). Holiness is one of the key factors that separates ministry leaders from other leaders. Ministry leaders must align their beliefs and actions with the moral tenets of God as revealed in God's Word. Righteousness is something God gives us—holiness is something we choose. Leaders choose to walk and live holy.

Practicing or continuing in sin blocks a Christian's fellowship with God, affects his or her relationship with other believers, and diminishes his or her Christian witness. Confession and repentance must become disciplines of the Christian leader's life. Christian leaders must demonstrate a lifestyle that is based on Scripture and provides a witness to the life-changing power of the gospel. Where we go, where we "hang out," reflects who we are and our inner motivations. As we grow in Christ, our lifestyle comes more and more to reflect that of Christ. Our words and actions begin to line up more and more with those of Christ.

Review statements 31-35 on the SWI and mark those you scored a 4 or 5. Use a different mark to indicate those questions you scored a 1 or 2.

Wisdom

See then that you walk circumspectly, not as fools, but as wise,
Redeeming the time, because the days are evil. ~Ephesians 5:15-16

Wise, judicious decision-making is evidence of a healthy Christian walk, manifests in every area of the believer's life, and enables the believer to stay focused on God's agenda. Christian leaders must daily make choices and decisions. These choices and decisions must emanate from a mature and maturing relationship with the Lord in which God's wisdom and mind are revealed to the leader.

Procrastination, distraction, and misplaced priorities diminish the Christian leader's effectiveness and ultimately hinder his or her service. Hasty, unwise, and impulsive decisions detract from the Christian leader's walk and cause leaders to overcommit, over-function, and lose balance. There is a direct correlation between poor self-care and unwise or poor decision-making. When we are frazzled, hurt, angry, tired, and weary, our minds and hearts our cloudy and we are less tuned in to the Holy Spirit, or our deeply settled inner-wisdom. It's when we are coping with some type of hurt or rejection that some of us amass entire new wardrobes, max out our credit cards, end otherwise godly relationships, or enter into otherwise obviously unhealthy relationships. Let's look at the questions in this category again. Notice self-care, balance, and wise scheduling of time are all choices that you make; at a deep level they are spiritual choices. Wisdom comes from God (James 1:5) and with maturity.

Review statements 36-40 in the SWI and mark those you scored a 4 or 5. Use a different mark to indicate those questions you scored a 1 or 2.

Practices for Strengthening Your Spiritual Walk
Using the Spiritual Walk Inventory™ reflect on the following points as you seek God about your Spiritual Walk.

(1) Build your faith in God. (statements 1-5)

a) Acknowledge/affirm your faith—God has dealt to each one a measure of faith (Romans 12:3)
b) Read, study, meditate on, and confess the Word of God—faith cometh by hearing and hearing by the word of God (Romans 10:17)
c) Pray—But you beloved, building yourselves up on your most holy faith, praying in the Holy Spirit (Jude 20)

d) Fight the good fight of faith—you build up your faith "muscles" every time you use your faith (1 Timothy 6:12)

(2) Cultivate spiritual sensitivity. (statements 6-10)

a) Totally surrender your heart to God— *Since, then, you have been raised with Christ, set your hearts on things above, where Christ is seated at the right hand of God. Set your minds on things above, not on earthly things.* (Colossians 3:1-2)
   a. Confession of sin; repentance and turning away from sinful, carnal behaviors
   b. Confession of faults to one another (e.g., trusted confidante, accountability partner, prayer partner)
b) Engage in regular and consistent spiritual disciplines (see Chapter 11 for a description)— *Seek the LORD and his strength, seek his face continually* (1 Chronicles 16:11)
   a. Inward Disciplines
   b. Outward Disciplines
   c. Corporate Disciplines
c) Remain open and aware to the presence of God in every situation— *Where can I go from your Spirit? Where can I flee from your presence? If I go up to the heavens, you are there; if I make my bed in the depths, you are there.* (Psalm 139:7-8, NIV)

(3) Gain insight into God's purpose for you. (statements 11-15)

a) Believe that God has a plan and purpose for your life. (Jeremiah 29:11; Ephesians 2:11)
b) Seek to know your purpose through prayer and worship. Ask God to reveal His purposes for you. As you draw closer to the Lord through prayer and worship, you increase your ability to hear what the Lord has to share with you on His purposes for you.(Matthew 6:33)
c) Read books on purpose. (Proverbs 18:15)
d) Take assessments (e.g., Spiritual Gifts Assessments). A spiritual gift assessment will not tell you what your spiritual gift is, but it will give you a starting point for exploring through prayer, service, and counsel the ways in which you have been spiritually gifted. Better understanding into your own gifting provides a place to start praying about your purposes to serve.
e) Observe, experience, and reflect. Start working or serving in an assigned area. Prayerfully reflect on your sense of fulfillment and purpose.

(4) Enhance your character. (statements 16-20)

a) Learn and practice healthy spirituality that integrates the emotions and the spirit, the mind, and the heart. (Mark 12:30)
b) Enhance your self-awareness and grow in authenticity. (Philippians 3:12-14)
c) Move from talking at God to being with God. (Psalm 84)
d) Move from a mere activity-based identity to a being/becoming identity. (John 15:15)
e) Move from self-centeredness to Christ-centeredness. (Luke 9:23; Galatians 2:20)

(5) Cultivate love. (statements 21-25)

a) Reflect on and be constrained by the love of Christ. (2 Corinthians 5:14)
b) Repent of unloving, hateful ways. (Psalm 139:23-24)
c) Ask God to love through you. (1 John 4:7-11)
d) Ask God to heal the broken places in you that block your ability to love and forgive. (Psalm 147:3)

(6) Maintain unity. (statements 26-30)

a) Examine your own attitude and guard against attitudes of strife. (Romans 1:28-32; 13:11-14; 1 Corinthians 1:1-4).
b) Examine how you speak to fellow ministry members (what you say and how you say things; your tone and manner of speech can build others up or tear them down). (Proverbs 12:18; Philippians 2:14; Proverbs 11:13; Ephesians 4:29)
c) Commit to guard the unity of your ministry. (Ephesians 4:1-3)
d) Commit to deal with conflict in healthy ways. (Ephesians 4:26)

(7) Practice holiness. (statements 31-35)

a) Understand God's definition of holiness, what it means to possess moral authority and commit to holy living. (Romans 12:1-2)
b) Choose activities that nourish your spirit and bring glory to God. (Colossians 3:17)
c) Refrain from activities that do not build up your spirit and do not bring glory to God. (1 Corinthians 10:23)

(8) Make wiser choices. (statements 36-40)

a) Ask God for wisdom. (Ephesians 1:17; James 1:5)

b) Seek input and perspectives from a "multitude of counselors."
(Proverbs 11:4; 15:22)

c) Learn from past mistakes. (Luke 15:18; Psalm 119:77; Philippians 3:13)

d)Do not beat yourself up. Forgive, let go, and move on. (Psalm 3:3)

Leadership spirituality is critical to effective church leadership. Leaders who value the life of the Spirit and seek to hear God lead from a powerful *dunamis* base. Because transformation is about being changed from the inside out, transformative leaders must be changed from the inside out, and they must be able to help others along the transformative journey.

Chapter 11—Reflection

1. How has your personal spiritual walk impacted the way you serve and lead in ministry?

2. How closely linked are your calling and purpose and what you do in ministry?

3. Give an example or two of how some of the spiritual qualities unpacked in this chapter impact your service and leadership in a positive way. Write those examples next to your higher scoring spiritual qualities.

   Faith:
   Spiritual Sensitivity:
   Purpose:
   Godly Character:
   Love:
   Unity:
   Holiness:
   Wisdom:

4. For the spiritual qualities you didn't score as high in, how can you begin to cultivate or strengthen those qualities in both your personal walk and your service to God and His people? Write your answers next to those qualities below.

   Faith:
   Spiritual Sensitivity:
   Purpose:
   Godly Character:
   Love:
   Unity:
   Holiness:
   Wisdom:

Spiritual disciplines are means of enhancing the believer's spiritual sensitivity and ability to remain open to the heart and voice of God. In *A Celebration of Discipline*, a classic text on spiritual disciplines, Richard Foster states that the spiritual disciplines are "means of receiving God's grace. …[They] allow us to place ourselves before God so [God] can transform us."[1]

A spiritual discipline is a practice that when engaged in on a regular basis helps to focus a believer on God and the things of God, and it opens a believer to hear what God is saying. The purpose of spiritual disciplines is to transform a person by "replac[ing] old destructive habits of thought with new life-giving habits."[2]

Sometimes called spiritual practices, the disciplines are not intended to become perfunctory activities engaged in for the purposes of checking the box on things we've completed on our spiritual to-do list. Instead, they are the means by which God builds disciples and ultimately leaders. Thus, in building a Church Full of Leaders, there is a wonderful interplay between disciplines, discipleship, and leadership. There lies the marvelous opportunity for pastors and equippers to help transform followers into disciples and disciples into leaders and agents of change. Clearly, transformation is the work of the Holy Spirit. Yet God enlists us in the marvelous process of transformation—changing our mind-sets, our hearts, and ultimately growing us up!

In *Spiritual Formation*, Henri Nouwen writes, "Discipleship… calls for discipline. Indeed, discipleship and discipline share the same linguistic root (from *discere,* which means 'to learn from') and the two should never be separated."[3] Nouwen goes on to give insight into the various disciplines of the spiritual life of the disciple such as prayer, meditation, solitude, and silence.

Discipline for the disciple is like water to a fish. It's part of what just is for us, what is natural. It's what we do as part of who we are—ideally. In reality, we don't always get it right. At times we overeat. We spend too much money. We talk too much. Sometimes we get caught up in the excesses of the culture. The latent compulsions rise to the surface and demand our attention.

Yet in these times the disciple must yield to the call back to God, away from the noise. Away from the hustle and bustle and back to the disciplines that bring discipline to every dimension of our lives. In that way, even in our most undisciplined state, the true disciple learns. We learn that the deepest longings of our hearts cannot be filled with things. We learn God has a way of disciplining us that brings us back from the brink of excess. Thus, we learn that we cannot truly be disciplined followers of Christ without the grace of God and the help of the Holy Spirit.

For some, discipline without discipleship is said to be rigid formalism. For the Christian, there is no discipleship without discipline. Whether the discipline we enact or the discipline God exacts, the life of the Christ follower is a lifelong journey of learning. And growing. And being transformed.

Foster provides three categories: inward disciplines, outward disciplines, and corporate disciplines. Let's take a look at each category.

The Inward Disciplines

- **Meditation upon the Word.** The practice of reflectively pondering and carefully attending to a word or passage of Scripture in order to receive revelation from God's Word (Joshua 1:8; Psalm 1:2; 1 Timothy 4:15)

- **Prayer.** The practice of conversing with God in order for the Spirit to shape our hearts and mold our wills (Luke 11:1; Luke 18:1)

- **Fasting.** The practice of abstaining from food and/or drink for spiritual purposes (Isaiah 58:6)

- **Study.** The practice of studying Scripture for the renewing of the mind (2 Timothy 2:15)

The Outward Disciplines

- **Simplicity.** The practice of simplifying one's life and possessions to both reflect an inner attitude and to guard against idolatry (Luke 16:13; Philippians 4:12)

- **Solitude.** The practice of sitting quietly or silently before God with an inner emptiness, expecting God to speak (Ecclesiastes 3:7; Matthew 26:36-46; Mark 1:35; Luke 6:12)

- **Submission.** The practice of "letting go" of our stubborn self-will and embracing God's will (Matthew 10:39; Mark 8:34)

- **Service.** The practice of serving people out of an agape love ethic or motive (Matthew 23:11)

The Corporate Disciplines

- **Confession of the Word of God.** The practice of confessing (or speaking the same thing) about oneself, a situation or a biblical promise as God would (Romans 10:10; Hebrews 4:12)

- **Worship.** The practice of experiencing the presence of God (Matthew 4:10; John 4:23-24)

- **Guidance.** The practice of seeking and receiving direction both personally and corporately (Acts 13:2; 15)

- **Celebration.** The practice of rejoicing and praising God (Psalm 11; John 15:11; 1 Thessalonians 5:16)

The purpose of this handbook is not to recap Foster's typology; I encourage you to pick up his book for that. In the next few chapters, however, we will explore a few of the spiritual disciplines that are particularly vital to church leaders. These disciplines help church leaders stay open to the Spirit, cultivate the discipline necessary for leading, and keep the heart open to the people we serve and serve with. Before we explore three leadership disciplines in detail (prayer, the Word, and quiet time), let's close this chapter with tips for incorporating the spiritual disciplines into our lives.

Closing Tips: Incorporating Spiritual Disciplines into the Lives of Ministry Leaders

Leaders are typically high energy, super busy multi-taskers. Ministry leaders are no exception. If ministry leaders are not careful, they can become so busy and caught up in the programming and executing of ministry that they fail to attend to the heart of ministry—especially their own hearts—as it relates to the heart of God. Following are some ways ministry leaders can incorporate the spiritual disciplines into their busy lives:

- **Slow down.** The trick of the enemy is to keep us so busy and moving at such a fast past, that our spiritual ears become dull and our hearts hardened. In our hurriedness, our inner selves become harried; it becomes evident in the ways in which we interact with each other—impatiently, rudely, curtly, and so on. We become victims of the urgent and fail to prioritize what is truly important. Commit to revisiting your schedule and carving out time for spiritual disciplines.

- **Develop a rhythm of spiritual practices or disciplines** such that spending time with God and positioning yourself to hear from God becomes your lifestyle.

- **Set a goal.** Start with setting a modest goal of 15 minutes a day for prayer and devotional reading, and increase that commitment as your thirst for your time with God increases. Honor that time as your appointment time with God and don't cancel it. You may have to get up a little earlier, before the rest of the family. Or you may choose to have devotional time with your spouse and/or children.

- **Be consistent.** Just as an athlete develops the discipline of consistently training for his or her sport or a musician develops the discipline to consistently practice to hone his or her craft, so must we consistently partake in and live out the spiritual disciplines. As the old adage goes, "Consistency is the mark of the true champion." We are spiritual champions, so let's live it out.

- **Study the spiritual disciplines.** Learn the ancient practices of the church and seek God about the particular or specific disciplines you need to structure into your life.

- **Secure a good devotional Bible.** Devotional reading of Scripture, or even of a devotional book, will allow you to read with the intent of devoting your whole heart to hearing from God through the Scriptures. Find a translation of the Bible that matches your learning and reading style so that you can read with understanding. A number of devotional books provide a daily Scripture reading and a reflection upon that Scripture.

- **Find a personal prayer method.** More will be said about prayer for leaders in the next chapter.

Chapter 12—Reflection

Review the list of spiritual disciplines. From each category, select a discipline and describe a way ministry leaders can strive to encourage the development of that discipline through ongoing servanthood training/development.

Inward:

Outward:

Corporate:

As ministry leaders, we know the importance of prayer—we pray for the congregation and members of our ministries who are in need. But as our lives become busier and busier, sometimes maintaining a consistent discipline of prayer becomes problematic.

Yet, thankfully, God continually beckons us to come to Him. He relentlessly pursues our hearts, inviting us to commune with Him daily. Our communion draws us closer to Him, strengthening our faith and our resolve to live for and serve Him, and keeps us ever mindful of the true purpose of our leadership—to bring glory to the One who loves us dearly.

As ministry leaders we sometime need a refresher on prayer to get us back into the habit of praying. In this chapter we provide an approach to prayer that can help new ministry leaders build a prayer life and allow seasoned ministry leaders to strengthen theirs.

Biblical Models of Prayer

Let's start with the models the Lord gives us in Scripture.

Jesus, Our Example in Prayer

Jesus, our Lord and Savior, in His earthly walk, is our chief example of one who prayed. He arose early for private prayer (Mark 1:35). After the miracle of the feeding, He went aside to pray alone (Matthew 14:23). He was praying when the Holy Spirit came to Him at His baptism (Luke 3:21). He had spent the whole night in prayer before He chose the Twelve (Luke 6:12, 13). Luke says that the transfiguration occurred "as he was praying" (9:28, 29); prayer carried Him through Gethsemane, "where he prayed in agony" (Luke 22:44); and His last words on the cross were a prayer.

Our Eternal Prayer Assistance

In John 17, we read that Jesus prayed for us in what is now known as His High Priestly Prayer; and in Hebrews 7:25, we are reminded that Jesus always lives to make intercession for us. Paul reminded us in Romans 8:26-27, "Likewise the Spirit also helps us in our weaknesses. For we don't know what to pray for as we ought, but the Spirit Himself makes intercession for us with groanings which cannot be uttered. Now He who searches the hearts knows what the mind of the Spirit is, because He makes intercession for the saints according to the will of God."

A Legacy of a Praying Church

The church was birthed out of a prayer meeting, as the 120 believers met in the upper room waiting for the promised Holy Spirit. Prayer kept them on one accord (Acts 1, 2). The disciples prayed for guidance for church life (Acts 1;24, 6:6, 13:3, 14:23). Prayer was something the New Testament Christian did daily (Acts 2:42). Believers met at Mary's house and prayed for Peter's deliverance from prison (Acts 12:5), and Paul and Silas prayed while in prison (Acts 16:25).

As we see, prayer was important to or Lord and His first leaders and therefore is important to us, leaders in his church today.

The Principle of Prayer

As leaders, many of us often like to think of ourselves as being in control. Though we have some control, we don't have all control. As we begin to refresh and strengthen our praying, we must remember a key principle that will make our praying more effective. God is in control, we're not. God is all powerful—not us. God is all knowing, not us. God is always working, even when we can't. And God knows what to do, even when we don't. Sometimes as leaders we want to tell God what to do. But prayer is an avenue for each of us to be strengthened in our desire for God's will to be done in our lives and in our leading.

We also have to remember that God loves us even when we don't feel loved or appreciated by the people we serve. God can hear the quietest cries of our hearts when we can't talk to another solitary soul. God loves the people for whom we are praying and whom we lead even when we don't seem to understand them. And we have to remember that the aim of prayer is not to complain to God about the people, but to know that we can commune with Him even when we feel most vulnerable from the many demands of ministry leadership. As ministry leaders, we have the awesome privilege of communing with God through prayer, as He guides us in living and leading.

Getting Started—Again

Prayer is a dialogic discipline—the practice of dialoguing with God through the conversation of the heart. We don't have to acquire a new vocabulary per se of fancy, religious-sounding words. We can talk to God straight from our hearts about the issues we are facing, the things we are feeling. We can talk to God about our deepest desires, our fears, our hopes, and our dreams. We can also sit quietly and wait on God, listening for His voice and words of wisdom, His guidance, and His comfort. That is the power of prayer—we can communicate with God. We tell the people of our ministries just these points but sometimes forget to remind ourselves!

As we begin to reignite a consistent practice of personal praying, there are a few items we may want to secure to help us to settle into personal praying.

- **Notebook/Journal or Prayer App** to record prayer requests, answered prayers, or just the "doodlings" of the heart. We can keep prayer lists in this journal—reminding us of others for whom to pray. We can jot down major life decisions in this journal and then refer to these lists when making specific requests of God. We can pray for guidance and direction on these life decisions.
- **Quiet Place** to provide uninterrupted space with God. In this quiet time, we can empty the rumblings of our hearts. We can turn off the telephone or turn down the ringer and sit or lie quietly in a comfortable place such as the bedroom. Some people carve out this quiet space at the kitchen table. Others mark out their quiet space in the bathroom, perhaps even in a hot tub of water. Some people arrive at their offices early—before the busyness starts—and sit quietly at their desks. Some parents arise early in the morning and spend their quiet time before the children get up.
- **Worship Music** to help set the tone and create an atmosphere conducive for prayer and worship of the almighty God. Some people sit quietly and just listen to a CD of quiet, soul-stirring worship music.

A Process for Praying

In our early formative years, many of us may have learned to use the prayer process ACTS as a means for structuring our prayers. Sometimes seasoned ministry leaders have gotten so busy with life and leading they have lapsed in regular disciplined prayer time may need to return to this process to get back on the track of daily disciplined praying. Another helpful model for praying is provided in *Praying to Change Your Life: A Guide to Productive Prayer* by Suzette T. Caldwell (Destiny Image Press, 2009). For now, here's a quick refresher on the ACTS prayer model.

ACTS

Adoration. First we start our prayer with adoration and worship of God. During this time, we can just worship God for who God is. We don't have to ask for anything or do anything—just worship God, calling to mind the attributes and qualities of God. God is the Creator of the universe, the Sovereign God. We may call to mind Bible verses that extol God or we might just use our own words of appreciation for God and the relationship that we have with the almighty God, King of Kings, and Lord of Lords!

Confession. During this time in our prayer, we take the time to confess to God our own sinfulness—even, your specific sin. Different from confessing the Word, this confession is an emptying of our sinful hearts before God. There's no need trying to hold this stuff in our hearts or minds. Christ died for our sin—everyone one of them: past, present, and future. The guilt of sin was transferred at the cross of Calvary. Too often we hold on to our own sin and live lives of condemnation. Romans 8:1-2 states, "There is therefore now no condemnation to those who are in Christ Jesus because the law of the Spirit of life has set me free from the law of sin and death" (NIV). First John 1:8 suggests that we deceive ourselves if we claim to be without sin. Too often, in our efforts to live the "perfect" Christian life, especially as ministry leaders, we bury our sin deep within the recesses of our mind and then are plagued with vague feelings of guilt. John assures us that "if we confess our sins, he is faithful and just and will forgive us our sins and purify us from all unrighteousness" (1 John 1:9). God is faithful to forgive us our sins based on the atoning work of Jesus Christ. Prayers of confession allow us to be honest with God about who we really are and what we struggle with. In being honest with God, we begin to be honest with ourselves. Finally, confession gives us the opportunity to affirm our need for God, reminding our independent, strong-willed selves that we need God.

Thanksgiving. During this time of prayer, we thank God for what He has done for us! We thank God for our blessings. Before we take any specific requests to God, we thank Him for what He has already done. Prayers of thanksgiving cultivate within us an "attitude of gratitude." They teach us "in everything [to] give thanks for this is the will of God in Christ Jesus" (1 Thessalonians 5:18). The apostle Paul intertwined thanksgiving into many of his prayers and in his teaching. "Thanks be unto God! He gives us the victory through our Lord Jesus Christ" (1 Corinthians 15:58). "Now thanks be to God who always leads us in triumph in Christ" (2 Corinthians 2:14). "Thanks be to God for His indescribable gift" (2 Corinthians 9:15). We can think of everything we have to be grateful for and begin to express our thankfulness to God.

Supplication. To supplicate just means to "ask humbly and earnestly." During this time of prayer, we make our requests to God. This is the time for making our specific requests known to God. It may be helpful to write these requests down in our journal or notebook or enter into our prayer app. We can pray expecting God to answer our prayers, and later come back to these entries and note when and how God answered

our prayers. We must always remember, even when asking God, we pray "according to the will of God" for ourselves and for others.

Admittedly, as we mature and grow in our relationship with the Lord, our prayer life matures from a scripted set of guidelines to a fluid conversation with God, directed by the Holy Spirit. As prayer becomes a habit, a regular disciplined conversation between us and God guided by the Holy Spirit, we may relinquish the above method as we come more and more to be directed by the Holy Spirit as to what to pray. As leaders, our prayer lives must be such that we can talk to and listen to God; we can attune our spiritual ears and hearts to the voice of the Spirit.

Prayer Assignment

Take some time right now to develop an action plan to put these points into use. Where in your home can you carve out some quiet space to pray on a regular basis? What adjustments to your schedule and/or your family's schedule do you need to make to schedule a regular time of prayer? When can you buy or locate an unused notebook to use as a prayer tool?

Remember, it will be most beneficial for you to develop a regular and consistent time of prayer. Make praying a habit—and it takes about seven days for a habit to stick. Determine this week to pray on a regular basis, using the principles found in this first lesson. Set a reasonable daily goal for yourself such as setting aside ten minutes of regular, consistent praying. As praying becomes a habit and your relationship with God is enhanced, you will want to pray more—and will find more time to pray.

Why We Pray

God gave us prayer so we could have conversation with Him, but we often distort this by "saying prayers" and hurrying off without ever listening to what is on our Father's heart.
~Experiencing God Day-By-Day Devotional

After getting started again with prayer, we'll want to remind ourselves why we pray. It sounds simple, but understanding the purpose of any endeavor helps us become more effective in that endeavor. And to really become effective in prayer, we must go back to the Bible to get critical insights on why we pray. Here are nine reasons why we pray:

1. We pray to discover God's will. We pray to discover God's purpose, plans, and priorities for our lives. God has a plan for our lives, and we pray to seek God's will and make His will our priority. Through prayer we seek God's "agenda."

For I know the plans that I have for you, says the Lord. They are plans for good and not for disaster to give you a future and a hope. ~Jeremiah 29:11, NLT

The Lord will work out his plans [promises and purposes] for my life—for your faithful love, O Lord, endures forever. ~Psalm 138:8, NLT

Being confident of this very thing, that He who has begun a good work in [me] will complete it until the day of Jesus Christ. ~Philippians 1:6, NKJV
For it is God who works in [me] both to will and to do of His good pleasure. ~Philippians 2:13, NKJV

Show me Your ways, O Lord; Teach me your paths; Lead me in Your truth and teach me. ~Psalm 25:4, 5, NKJV

Trust in the Lord with all thine heart; and lean not unto thine own understanding. In all thy ways acknowledge him, and he shall direct thy paths. ~Proverbs 3:5, 6, KJV

We can gather our thoughts, but the Lord gives the right answer. ~Proverbs 16:1, NLT

Commit [my] work to the Lord, and then [my] plans will succeed. ~Proverbs 16:3, NLT

2. We pray to access spiritual resources. We have access through the Spirit to spiritual resources. Through prayer we can access these spiritual resources.

...that the God of our Lord Jesus ... may give you the spirit of wisdom and revelation in the knowledge of him. ~Ephesians 1:17, NKJV
The peace of God, which surpasses all understanding, will guard your hearts and minds through Christ Jesus. ~Philippians 4:7, NKJV

Through (Jesus) also we have access by faith into this grace in which we stand. ~Romans 5:2, NKJV

Let us therefore come boldly to the throne of grace, that we may obtain mercy and find grace to help in time of need. ~Hebrews 4:16, NKJV

3. We pray to release our fear and anxiety.

Cast your cares on the Lord and he will sustain you. ~Psalm 55:22, NIV
Be anxious for nothing, but in everything through prayer and supplication with thanksgiving let your request be made known to God. ~Philippians 4:6, NKJV

4. We pray to intercede on behalf of others.

…prayers, intercessions and giving of thanks be made for all men, for kings and for all who are in authority, that we may lead a quiet and peaceable life in all godliness and reverence.
~1 Timothy 2:1, 2, NKJV

5. We pray to bring down strongholds in our minds.
We pray to bring our thought life into obedience to Christ. Strongholds, or walls of doubt, disbelief, and disobedience, can be established in our own mind. We pray for God to penetrate these walls and bring our thoughts in line with God's mind.

For the weapons of our warfare are not carnal but mighty through God to the pulling down of strongholds, casting down arguments and every high thing that exalts itself against the knowledge of God, bringing every thought into captivity to the obedience of Christ. ~2 Corinthians 10:4-5, NKJV

For God has not given us the spirit of fear but of power and of love and of a sound mind. ~2 Timothy 1:7

6. We pray to combat the forces of darkness.

Finally my brethren, be strong in the Lord and in the power of His might. Put on the whole armor of God…praying with all prayer and supplication in the Spirit. ~Ephesians 6:10-18, NKJV

7. We pray to express our deepest need for God.

For in Him we live and move and have our being. ~Acts 17:28

8. We pray to ask God for our needs to be met.

And my God shall supply all your need according to His riches in glory by Christ Jesus. ~Philippians 4:19, NKJV

9. We pray to experience the presence of God. We pray to fellowship and commune with our Creator, our Savior, our Redeemer, our Lord!

> *In Your presence is fullness of joy; at Your right hand are pleasures forevermore.* ~Psalm 16:11, NKJV

The Posture of Prayer

Prayer is a universal phenomenon in which people the world over cry out to God. People pray differently. Various cultures approach prayer differently. Some people kneel down, outwardly showing the inner humility of their heart. Some people stand, with arms outstretched. They implore God, reaching out to God to connect with the Almighty.

Some people lie down on the floor, prostrate with face to the floor. They physically lower themselves in quiet submission to God. Some people sit, resting and waiting upon God—some on the side of the bed, some at the kitchen table, some at the lakefront, on the beach, or in the mountains. Some people in fast-paced societies commune with and communicate with God while seated on the bus, the train, or airplane. Some people talk to God as they walk, run, jog, or exercise. And some pray in the comfort of a hot tub of water.

In some cultures, people pray upon prayer mats. In some cultures, people who pray don prayer shawls. In some cultures, there are designated times of the day in which one must pray. In some cultures there are restrictions on praying; people are persecuted for professing Christ—as well as for praying to Him. In other cultures, one can pray at any time, with no special equipment, tools, techniques, or garments. Regardless of our prayer traditions, we are blessed that we have the privilege to pray to God, who always hears us.

More important than our physical posture, however, is our inner posture toward God and toward prayer. Our inner posture refers to our mind-set, our perspective, and our attitude. The following Scriptures can help us develop a powerful prayer posture.

1. Pray in agreement with a "prayer partner," knowing that God will answer our prayers.

Assuredly, I say unto you, whatever you bind on earth will be bound in heaven, and whatever you loose on earth will be loosed in heaven. Again I say to you that if two of you agree on earth concerning anything that they ask, it will be done for them by My Father in heaven. ~Matthew 18:19

2. Pray in faith and forgiveness. Believe that we will receive the things for which we ask.

Have faith in God. For assuredly I say to you, whoever says to this mountain, "be removed and be cast into the sea" and does not doubt in his heart, but believes that

those things which he says will be done, he will have whatsoever he says. Therefore I say to you, whatever things you ask when you pray, believe that you receive them and you shall have them. ~Mark 11:22-25

3. Pray boldly and consistently. Jesus alludes to our "importunity"—our persistence in prayer.

So I say to you, ask, and it will be given to you; seek and you will find; knock, and it will be opened to you. For everyone who asks receives, and he who seeks finds, and to him who knocks it will be opened. ~Luke 11:9, 10

4. Pray according to the Word. If we "stay in the Word," our desires begin to be shaped by the Word— God's will and way. We come to want what God wants for us.

If you abide in Me, and My words abide in you, you shall ask what you desire and it shall be done for you. ~John 15:17

5. Pray confidently, according to the will of God.

Now this is the confidence that we have in Him, that if we ask anything according to His will, He hears us. And if we know that He hears us, whatever we ask, we know that we have the petitions that we have asked of Him. ~1 John 5:14-15

Remember, prayer is not a mental exercise in futility—it is a real experience with the real God. Find a physical position that is comfortable for you, perhaps at your desk at work or perhaps in your home. Read one of the above Scriptures in its entirety and reflect upon it. Then go to God in prayer, in your powerful new prayer posture.

Praying the Word

A classic book on prayer is *Praying the Scriptures: Communicating with God in His Own Words*, by Judson Cornwall. In it, among other things, the author shows how the Scriptures initiate us to prayer, invite us to prayer, and involve us in prayer. Sometimes, he even says the Scriptures become the ingredients of our prayer.[1]

For ministry leaders, it's helpful to review actual prayers written in the Bible. These were prayers uttered by various people in Scripture and the Holy Spirit included those prayers in Scripture for our edification and use. One example we will explore comes from the pen and mouth of the apostle Paul. Many scholars consider the following passage to be an actual prayer that Paul uttered on behalf of his readers.

I keep asking that the God of our Lord Jesus Christ, the glorious Father, may give you the Spirit of wisdom and revelation, so that you may know him better. I pray that the eyes of your heart may be enlightened in order that you may know the hope to which he has called you, the riches of his glorious inheritance in his holy people, and his incomparably great power

for us who believe. That power is the same as the mighty strength he exerted when he raised Christ from the dead and seated him at his right hand in the heavenly realms (Ephesians 1:17-20, NIV).

To turn this passage into a personal prayer, lets insert the personal pronoun where appropriate. A personalized prayer from this passage may sound like this:

Father, may You give me the Spirit of wisdom and revelation, so that I may know You better. I pray also that the eyes of my heart may be enlightened in order that I may know the hope to which You have called me, the riches of Your glorious inheritance in the saints, and Your incomparably great power for us who believe. That power is like the working of Your mighty strength, which You exerted in Christ when You raised Him from the dead and seated Him at Your right hand in the heavenly realms.

As you can see, praying the Word can be a deeply moving and personal practice as we are specifically seeking God for things for ourselves right out of God's Word. Praying the Word is a powerful means of praying and building up our faith. Praying the Word can be a deeply moving and personal practice as we are specifically seeking God for things for ourselves right out of God's Word.

A Final Word on Prayer

Earlier we referred to prayer as the "dialogic discipline." We've spent some time in this chapter getting you started with the dialogue—reminding you of the preciousness of the communion with God that comes through prayer. Yet, in addition to our talking to God, is the awesome experience of hearing from God—even listening for God.

Part of the communing with God is waiting on the Lord and listening for God's answers to our requests, or for God's direction, or for God's loving whispers of comfort. As we develop more and more of our prayer discipline, we can carve out time of silence and quietness to still the voices demanding our attention and to empty our minds of the hubbub of the work in order to listen to the still small voice of the Spirit.

Closing Tips: As you prepare to make prayer a priority, here are some tips that may be of value to you:

- Expect to hear from God.
- Don't get discouraged when opposition arises. You are on the right track. Remember, Daniel prayed and God sent his answer immediately, but the forces of darkness held up his answer for 21 days. (Daniel 10:1-14)
- Review a prayer Scripture to help get started in your daily prayer time.

- Jot down your requests.
- Incorporate daily scripture reading before you pray into your devotional time.
- Review your prayer log and note how and when God answered your prayers.
- Accept God's answers to your prayers. Desire God's will, not yours.

As your church commits to build a Church Full of Leaders, aim to become a praying leader who joins with other leaders to establish a praying church. A praying church is a powerful church.

Chapter 13—Reflection

1. Have you ever used a method besides the ACTS model to provide guidance for your prayers? If so, describe it. How effective was it in helping prepare you to face the day or a particular situation about which you were praying?

2. Using the ACTS model, write a prayer seeking God's direction for:

    a. Your personal life
    b. The life of the ministry you lead
    c. The people who serve in the ministry you lead

3. Do you have a set time that you spend in prayer each day? If not, how might a daily "standing" appointment of prayer improve your communication and your relationship with the Father?

4. Find a prayer in the Bible and in the space below, personalize it as a prayer for yourself and a prayer of intercession for someone else.

Ministry leaders must be men and women of the Word. We must believe in the power of the Word of God to transform lives. We believe in preaching, teaching, and giving godly counsel from the Bible. We order our lives according to the precepts of Scripture. So why raise the topic of devotional Bible reading with ministry leaders—men and women who are supposedly seasoned in the Word of God?

First, because ministry leaders are busy people we are often the ones most tempted to let go of daily, disciplined Bible reading. We use the excuse that we study the Word of God to prepare our Bible lesson and sermons, or even to seek guidance and counsel for a member, as well as to provide guidance for equipping members of our ministries. Yet, using the Word of God as a tool for ministry activities is not the same as communing with God by listening for the Lord's heart and voice through His Word.

Next, because ministry leaders are often seasoned people, we are sometimes tempted to dismiss the importance and significance of daily, disciplined devotional Bible reading. We'll say, "I pray daily, but I don't set aside a regular time." And often because ministry leaders are seasoned and had developed a regular time of devotion in their early ministry life, they have now so incorporated those practices into their lives they don't set aside time each day, fully expecting that some time during the day they will read devotionally and pray. However, the subtle dilemma with this approach is that, because our lives have become so busy, and our schedules so full, that by not scheduling regular devotional time, we can too easily let other activities pile up on us throughout the day until we find ourselves at the end of the day out of time and too tired to spend quality devotional time with the Lord. Carving out daily devotional reading time takes discipline. Not doing so is much like saying, "Oh, I eat natural food daily, I just don't set aside regular time to eat."

Meditating on the Word of God

Meditating upon the Word of God is the practice of reflectively pondering and carefully attending to a word or passage of Scripture in order to receive revelation from God's Word (Joshua 1:8; Psalm 1:2; 1 Timothy 4:15).

In Scripture, meditating or mediation was a repetitive utterance of a phrase or words for the purpose of reinforcing a message and allowing it to get planted deep within the heart. Remember the psalmist prayed, "May the words of my mouth and the meditation of my heart be pleasing to you, O LORD, my rock and my redeemer (Psalm 19:14, NLT). In this context, meditation could also be translated thoughts or the words spoken to oneself.

When transitioning the children of Israel into the Promised Land after the death of Moses, God reassured Joshua, their new leader, that He would be with him and would bless him. And he instructed Joshua to study this book of instruction (or book of the law) continually, to meditate on it day and night (Joshua 1:8). Paul picked up this same method when instructing the fledgling leader Timothy, admonishing him to meditate or give careful attention to the things in which he had been instructed (1 Timothy 4:5). Meditating on the Word was to be a means of getting the Word into one's heart, and it can be likened unto ruminating and digesting the truths of Word so that the truths of the Word are internalized. When the truth of the Word was so internalized, it would become the guiding mechanism for Joshua as he led the people of God, as well as it was for Timothy. So it is with church leaders today, especially in a Church Full of Leaders. As more leaders are engaged in ministry and lead in alignment with the pastoral vision for the church, these leaders must be inculcated in the Word of God, not necessarily as Bible scholars but as people who read, reflect, and meditate on the Word of God for cultivating the ear to hear and the will to heed the will of God, and for reinforcing leadership messages.

Confessing the Word of God

Whereas meditating on the Word relates to words spoken within our heart, confessing the Word relates to words spoken out loud. Again, note how the psalmist in Psalm 19:4 admonished for both the word of our mouths and the meditations of our hearts to be acceptable to God. Note how Paul taught that with the mouth confession is made unto salvation and that with the heart a person believes unto righteousness. Belief starts in the heart and is confessed with the mouth. Every leader must understand the power of her or his words and how our words flow out of our belief systems to affect our world. Leaders who moan, groan, and complain create a world of chaos in ministry, whereas leaders who learn to confess the Word build up and activate their faith.

Confession in Scripture stems from the Greek *homologeo* {hom-ol-og-eh'-o} (e.g., Romans 10:9; Hebrews 11:13) and means "to say the same thing as another, i.e. to agree with, assent."[1] As a leadership practice, confessing the Word of God becomes speaking the Word of God, or truths from Scripture. Leaders may confess the Word to affirm the truth of their identity in Christ (e.g., "I am accepted in the beloved," Ephesians 1:6) or as a faith statement concerning a situation ("My God shall supply all my needs according to His riches in glory by Christ Jesus," Philippians 4:19). Furthermore, the adversary of our souls, the devil, will wage a battle against the children of God, particularly leaders. Using lies and deception, he lobs untruths into the mind to discourage and dissuade leaders. The wise leader recognizes this ploy and uses the Word of God to combat the lies of the devil.

Finally, how many of us can attest to the joy and edification that occurs when, as we regularly read the Word, a passage seems to jump off the page and speak directly to our situations. That dynamic, revelatory encounter with the Word cannot occur without a dynamic engagement with and in the Word.

Approaches to Devotional Reading

Daily devotional Bible reading is, therefore, a necessary discipline for leaders. It is not just for the new or growing saint, but it is also for mature believers—including church leaders. Daily devotional reading helps the believer stay attuned to the voice and heart of God. Just as daily eating nourishes the physical body, daily devotional reading and prayer help to nourish one's spirit and keep one in tune with the truth of God's Word. There are several approaches to daily devotional reading, two of which we will review in this handbook.

Bible Reading Plan

One approach to daily devotional reading is to use a daily Bible reading plan that entails reading a set number of verses or chapters a day. It may also entail reading an accompanying background commentary that gives background and exposition of the passages read. After reading the passages, the person reflects or meditates on the passages and what the words of Scripture mean for him or her or speak to a situation in his or her life. Some people answer a set of reflection questions and use a journal to record their responses and reflections.

Suggestions for securing a daily Bible reading plan include reading through the Gospels, reading through the Bible starting in Genesis, or reading through the New Testament. Some people read a Psalm a day, or read a chapter in Proverbs a day. Let the Holy Spirit guide you in developing the Bible reading plan that will be the most edifying to you during this season of your life. Use a translation of the Bible that helps you really engage with the text.

Devotional Book

Another valuable approach to daily devotional reading is to use a devotional book. The readings in devotional books can be organized by a common theme and can be included in the book by date or number. The devotional reading may include three elements: (1) a Scripture passage, (2) a reflective narrative on the passage, and (3) a closing prayer. Recommendations for devotional books are given in the resource section.

Our very own Scripture reminds us how important the Word of God is to believers, young and old (Psalm 119:9), proclaiming that he "hid the word in his heart" that he might not sin against God (119:11). Psalm 119, which is an ode to the Word of God, declares that "Forever, O LORD, Your word is settled in heaven (vs 8) and serves as a lamp to our feet and a light to our path" (v 105). In

other words, the Word of God comprises the guiding principles church leaders use to live by.

Growing leaders must commit to a regular discipline of reading, meditating, and confessing the Word of God. Ultimately, daily devotional reading helps the ministry leader cultivate the discipline of the Word of God. Bible reading and study, meditating on the Word, and confessing the Word are vital to building the leader's faith and increasing the leader's recognition of the will of God. The next section includes a couple of exercises to encourage leaders to begin the process of more consistently engaging in the Word of God.

Devotional Bible Reading—An Exercise

PASSAGE:
Now the Lord is the Spirit; and where the Spirit of the Lord is, there is liberty.
~2 Corinthians 3:17, NKJV

READ:
Read the assigned text several times. Read it in several different translations.

> *Now, the Lord is the Spirit, and wherever the Spirit of the Lord is, he gives freedom. (NLT)*

> *And when God is personally present, a living Spirit, that old, constricting legislation is recognized as obsolete. We're free of it! (The Message Bible)*

> *Now the Lord is the Spirit, and where the Spirit of the Lord is, there is liberty—emancipation from bondage, freedom. (The Amplified Bible)*

Read several passages above and/or below the passage to get the scriptural context.

> *Therefore, since we have such hope, we use great boldness of speech—unlike Moses, [who] put a veil over his face so that the children of Israel could not look steadily at the end of what was passing away. But their minds were blinded. For until this day the same veil remains unlifted in the reading of the Old Testament, because the [veil] is taken away in Christ. But even to this day, when Moses is read, a veil lies on their heart. Nevertheless when one turns to the Lord, the veil is taken away. Now the Lord is the Spirit; and where the Spirit of the Lord [is], there [is] liberty. But we all, with unveiled face, beholding as in a mirror the glory of the Lord, are being transformed into the same image from glory to glory, just as by the Spirit of the Lord. ~2 Corinthians 3:12–18, NKJV*

In the second or third reading of the passage and surrounding passages, pause on key words, phrases, or verses that speak to your heart, address an area of your life, or highlight God's characteristic, principle, or promise. Highlight or circle these key words or phrases that "speak" to you.

REFLECT:
- What is the context and meaning of this passage?
- What key words or phrases really speak to your heart?
- What is the Holy Spirit saying to you through this passage?
- How does this passage speak to your situation?
- What will you do in response to what you are hearing in this passage?

Chapter 14—Reflection

1. How consistent are you in daily devotional reading?

2. What things help or hinder your consistency?

3. What can you do to become more consistent in daily devotional reading?

4. In what ways can daily devotional reading strengthen not only your personal walk with the Lord but also your leadership in the church?

As leaders we can be so busy doing the work of the Lord that we lose sight of the Lord of the work. It doesn't help that we live in a culture of busyness—one that cultivates and promotes incessant activity, strident activism, and hyperactive connectivity. Our electronic devices keep us accessible to others 24 hours a day, 7 days a week. Talking heads on cable news shows and push notifications from news apps vie for our attention around the clock. Professionals are rewarded for the number of projects completed and sales closed, driving them to longer and longer hours. The ritual in the work world is to lament to coworkers about the long, demanding hours in a one-ups game to see who is the busiest, and by extension, who is perceived to be the most important. And this culture of busyness has crept into the church.

Pastoral leaders of small to medium-sized churches are often bi-vocational, working in the marketplace and serving in the church. Lay leaders are often busy professionals who give their time in serving the church atop demands at work and family responsibilities. Church leaders develop and launch program after program in an effort to build numbers, often at the expense of building healthy community. Evening and weekend ministry programs are run by people who have worked all day and all week. And every pastor knows Sunday, our congregational worship day, is really a "workday," as ministers teach, lead service, preach, and often schedule meetings in between and after services.

With all of this busyness, and the cacophony of our noisy lives, how can church leaders hear from God, in whose name we are serving and whose cause we are advancing? With schedules so full, when do leaders get to "be still" and know God? When does the Lord get to restore the souls of those running on the treadmill of life—seemingly going nowhere fast?

The restful discipline—Sabbath keeping—focuses us back on the Lord; and it creates the time and space to replenish our spirits, restore our souls, and rest our bodies. Without rest from our labor, leaders will begin to lead from a dry place, distant from the Lord of the work, disconnected from our true authentic selves, and disengaged from the people with whom we lead and who we serve.

The Sabbath Tradition

> *On the seventh day God had finished his work of creation,*
> *so he rested from all his work.*
> *~Genesis 2:2*

Jewish people the world over have observed Sabbath since antiquity and continue to do so in our contemporary society. Each week from sundown on

Friday to sundown on Saturday, they cease from their creating in honor of God, who ceased from His work on the seventh day of creation.

Buying, selling, merchandising, and trading are obvious forms of creating commerce, and Jewish shop owners close their stores early on Friday. Yet the ritual to cease from creating extends to even more mundane activities of life. Starting the elevator in a hotel, for instance, is seen as a form of creating a new current or cycle of energy. So for Sabbath keepers in some Jerusalem hotels, there is a bank of elevators that runs continuously and stop on each floor during the Sabbath so one does not have to push the button to his or her floor and start a new cycle of work.

Creating and working are replaced with prayer first and then the evening family meal. The Sabbath brings families together to remember God and each other.

Sabbath Keeping

Remember the Sabbath day, to keep it holy. Six days you shall labor and do all your work, but the seventh day is the Sabbath of the Lord your God. In it you shall do no work: you, nor your son, nor your daughter, nor your male servant, nor your female servant, nor your cattle, nor your stranger who is within your gates. For in six days the Lord made the heavens and the earth, the sea, and all that is in them, and rested the seventh day. Therefore the Lord blessed the Sabbath day and hallowed it. ~Exodus 20:8-11, NKJV

In ancient Israel, God commanded His people to "Remember the Sabbath." In this command, He set one day of the week apart from the other days, using His own cycle of work-rest as the pattern for His people to follow. The infinite Creator didn't need rest per se, but finite humans do, as does the rest of the created order. The budding fruitfulness of spring and summer is followed by the dormancy of winter. The activity of the daytime is followed by the quietness of night. Of course in our global economies work can be done around the clock, but the principle of the God instituted work-rest cycle remains.

Although honoring the Sabbath is part of the law, as a principle, Sabbath keeping transcends the law. Jesus said people were not created for the Sabbath, but the Sabbath for people (Mark 2:27). The Sabbath was created or instituted for us. Some prefer to call that set aside time "quiet time" or "down time," but some principles about Sabbath keeping can be helpful for us as we build a Church Full of Leaders. In our churches we need and want spiritually vibrant leaders.

Wayne Muller, in his book *Sabbath: Finding Rest, Renewal, and Delight in Our Busy Lives*, uses "Sabbath both as a specific practice and a larger metaphor, a starting point to invoke a conversation about the forgotten necessity of rest."[1] In

the Jewish tradition it is a holy day, the seventh day of the week. In the Christian tradition it is the first day of the week, the Lord's Day.

Yet Muller helps us to see Sabbath keeping not just as observing a special day, but as consecrating "a time to listen," as "a way of being in time where we remember who we are," and remember whose we are.[2] Sabbath is a time for sacred rest or as Ruth Haley Barton, in her book *Sacred Rhythms,* calls it "a sanctuary in time" to rest and delight in God. Sabbath keeping is sacred ritual.[3]

Sacred ritual points to something larger and is intended to help us remember and reflect on the holy. Sabbath keeping evokes a sacred memory of God's command and the continuity of the people of God. During Sabbath time, we remember the faithfulness of God to His people. We remember our bodies are temples of the Holy Spirit, a sacred site to God. We remember our connections to the people we serve. We remember that we are finite creatures ever in need of an infinite God.

Whether a weekend retreat, an annual sabbatical, or weekly Sabbath time, leaders need regular down time to unwind, rest, and recharge. And church leaders need to develop a sane ministry schedule that models for and encourages congregants to honor the sacred cycle of work-rest.

Letting Go

Initially when starting to incorporate Sabbath or intentional rest time into their schedules, busy leaders may begin to hyperventilate at the thought of slowing down, stopping and letting go of work, meetings, and program development. We tell ourselves it won't get done without us; and if we stop for even a moment, we'll get irretrievably behind or miss deadlines. Actually, very few things on our crammed to-do lists are matters of life and death; but, believe it or not, forging ahead without rest can be deadly—to ourselves, our churches and other leaders. Ruth Haley Barton gives a few pointers in what to let go of during Sabbath time.

Work. It will keep until you get back to it. For those who work traditional 9-to-5 jobs, weekend Sabbath time is in order. The temptation for ministers is to get all personal and family errands completed on Saturday and spend most of the day on Sunday in church activities. Pastors and ministry leaders have to be intentional in setting aside Sabbath time. Barton advises that we establish clear boundaries to protect Sabbath time. If we carve out an hour a day to work out and listen to worship music, then we should turn the devices off and have the office hold the calls.

Buying and Selling. Barton suggests that consumer activity can be excluded from the Sabbath. Commercial activity can distract us from the life-giving impulses of the sacred time of rest. Letting go of shopping includes resisting e-commerce!

Again, our devices are easy temptations to sneak in any little activity and spend some money.

Worry. Barton advises us to let go of "the emotional and mental hard work that we are engaged in all week long as we try to figure out everything in our life and make it all work."[4] As Jesus reminds us, "worrying is not going to add one inch to our frame." Nor is it going to solve our problems that call for the wisdom of God that can be best heard in a quieted soul.

Picking up Sacred Practices

Barton gives a simple answer for what we can replace busyness with on the Sabbath: "whatever delights you and replenishes you."[5]

Resting the body is essential. We can get rest by intentionally slowing down and by taking "a nap, a walk, a bike ride, a long bubble bath, eating your favorite foods, sitting in the sun, lighting candles, listening to beautiful music," and for married folks, "lovemaking."[6]

Sabbath is also for replenishing our spirits. Each of us must discover what replenishes the spirit. Replenishing the spirit is about re-energizing the core of who you are, giving space to make attitude adjustments, and reconnecting to purposeful pursuits. Reading a non work-related book, resting the mind through quiet time, painting, music, or solving puzzles helps revive the mind.

Restoring the soul is receiving "the deepest refreshment ... through worship and quiet music."[7] Devotional reading, prayer, journal writing, listening to worship music, and prayer walking are all restorative activities for Sabbath time.

Wayne Muller summarizes it best:

> *Sabbath is more than the absence of work; it is not just a day off, when we catch up on television or errands. It is the presence of something that arises when we consecrate period of time to listen to what is most beautiful, nourishing, or true. It is time consecrated with our attention, our mindfulness, honoring those quiet forces of grace or spirit that sustain and heal us."[8]*

Whether it's called Sabbath or quiet time, leaders who find the balance between work and rest, and intentionally incorporate the sacred time into their cycle of life, find they lead from a healthier, more spiritual place. It's as though as we slow down and experience the flow of the Spirit through us, we then lead from the overflow of that same Spirit. As we bask in the light of the Son, the light within our souls and spirits are recharged to shine more brightly for those around us.

Closing Tips

- Get started now—plan a time of Sabbath. Mark it in your calendar and keep the commitment for your soul's sake.
- Incorporate family members in your Sabbath time.
- Shift your measure of success from busyness and productivity to balance and fruitfulness. Help leaders who serve with you or on your team to do the same thing.
- Review your church or ministry calendar and take note of the cycles of your church life. Are there opportunities for balanced seasons of ministry activity and rest?

Chapter 15—Reflection

1. What challenges do you face in incorporating consistent, regular Sabbath time into your schedule?

2. Describe what happens when you lead on empty, without adequate rest?

3. How does the notion of a Church Full of Leaders actually facilitate more balanced living and leading (and hence time and space for Sabbath keeping) in your church?

4. What might you do to model Sabbath keeping for your church or ministry team?

Skill Building

E ncouraging believers to invest in their personal relationship with the Lord as a way of becoming stronger servants is important. Equipping them with concrete skills, like leading teams and running meetings effectively, as well as the less tangible skills they need to serve effectively, is just as important.

Equipping leaders for the work of ministry is critical to every church, especially in a Church Full of Leaders. As we have stated before in this manual, ministry is accomplished through people; and any leader who will lead ministry must develop the requisite skills for leading people in ministry.

What are those skills? So much of leadership is about relationship, and core skill sets necessary for ministry leadership center around working through relationships. Because ministry is done through people, skills of collaboration are essential. Being able to work with different personalities, being able to handle conflict without doing damage, and communicating well.

Some people believe leaders are born—they are gifted people who just have a way with other people. In actuality, the best leaders are those who have developed skills and competencies for leading. In fact, the skills that enhance leading churches are skills that enhance leadership in other venues such as work and home.

This final section shows leaders how to build within those who serve the skills they need to serve well.

Leadership as we have known it is shifting, undergoing its own transformation. The very idea of how we lead others is being transformed, coming back to the types of leadership that God ordained: leadership in which leaders engage in a process of collectively transforming God's people.

For every Moses, there was a Joshua, Caleb, Hur, Aaron, and Miriam. For every David, there was a team of mighty men of valor. For every Paul, there was a Barnabus, Silas, Timothy, Aquilla, Priscilla, and Phoebe. Even Jesus selected twelve men and surrounded Himself with women of influence to establish the church and extend the work of the kingdom of God. Biblical leadership was not an individualistic, transactional, isolated event but a collaborative, transformative, collective process in which leaders took on roles critical to achieving the aims and purposes of God.

Teams are vital to church, organizational, and denominational ministry. At its best, any large organization is really a set of well-organized teams. Individual leaders cannot accomplish the work of ministry alone. The body of Christ is an interconnected organism made up of cells and organs. In many ways, team in the contemporary church represents the cells of the body that function together to enable ministry to remain alive and well.

Although the term "team" is not found in the Bible, we do grasp in the Bible underlying principles that help today's leaders in forming and working with teams of people to accomplish the work of ministry.

Leaders Need Support to Carry Out Leadership Duties

According to Exodus 18:13, Moses held awesome leadership responsibilities for God's people—he helped the people seek God's will, resolved interpersonal conflicts, and taught the Word of God. These tasks were so great and the people so many, that the people stood before Moses from morning to evening. His was an all-day job! When Jethro, the priest of Midian and father-in-law to Moses saw what was happening, he asked Moses why he was trying to do it all by himself. As it was, the leadership task was too much for Moses alone. If Moses had continued the way he was going, the process would wear out him and the people!

Jethro might be considered the first executive coach, and like any good leadership coach, Jethro provided Moses with wise counsel—he gave Moses feedback on his current leadership practices, offered him an alternative that would be in the best interest of both the people and Moses, and left the choice to change up to Moses. Jethro suggested that Moses do two things:

- Focus his leadership on teaching the statutes and laws of God, showing the people the way in which they must walk and the work they must do
- Delegate the judging tasks to capable, God-fearing leaders of integrity

Moses had to broaden his leadership and invite other leaders to assist with the work of ministry in order that the work of ministry would be accomplished effectively and efficiently. Some of these leaders were leaders of thousands, some leaders of hundreds, some leaders of fifties, and some leaders of tens. These leaders are never identified as a team of leaders, yet this passage gives us keen insight into how other leaders provided some relief to Moses by assuming leadership responsibility of judging the people.

The effective leader in a Church Full of Leaders must focus on his or her own leadership responsibilities and tasks, and delegate other tasks to other leaders—this type of leadership collaboration is at the heart of teamwork.

Leaders Must Organize Others Who Work to Support the Ministry

Leaders need assistance in accomplishing great tasks, and that assistance must be organized into workable units in order to accomplish the tasks efficiently and effectively. God gave Nehemiah the vision to rebuild the walls of Jerusalem for the post-exilic community. Such was an awesome charge, and one that could not be accomplished by Nehemiah alone. Nehemiah organized the workers into about forty groups of workers who worked at the same time to build up or repair different sections of the city wall. As a leader, Nehemiah understood the importance of unified and coordinated work of these "teams" who worked side-by-side, working with brick and mortar and warding off physical and verbal attacks, so much so that he declared, "So we built the wall … for the people had a mind to work" (Nehemiah 4:6, NKJV).

Today's leaders, likewise, must organize men and women from throughout the congregation for the work of the ministry. Organizing people for ministry entails connecting them to the mission and vision of the ministry, properly placing them to serve, and releasing them to contribute their gifts, skills, and experiences for the ministry. Leaders who can do this will, like Nehemiah, garner commitment to the work and realize results.

Leaders Need the Power of the Collective to Change a System

Organizations and institutions are systems that get reinforced by the traditions and practices of many levels (and generations) of leaders and the people who interact in the system. Individuals do not change systems by themselves. The daughters of Zelophehad illustrate this principle for us. As the nation of Israel was on the brink of entering the Promised Land, and Moses was parceling out the plots of lands for each tribe and family, five sisters who would have been

excluded from inheriting land brought their concerns to Moses. The tradition required that land be handed down to men only. So if a "land-owning" man died and left no sons, his daughters could not inherit his land. According to Numbers 27:1-4, the five sisters approached Moses and the other leaders to petition them to allow their father's inheritance to pass to them. Moses took their issue before God and God said, "The daughters of Zelophehad speak what is right; you shall surely give them a possession of inheritance among their father's brothers, and cause the inheritance of their father to pass to them" (Numbers 27:7, NKJV).

God's pronouncement catalyzed Moses to sanction the daughters of Zelophehad to receive their father's inheritance, and thus set a precedent for inheritance laws in Israel, as well as for a great deal of the Western legal system. A group of women rallied together to challenge, and thus change, a system of traditions. Moving a church from traditional to a transformative Church Full of Leaders will take a collective, unified effort of leaders at every level.

Leaders Need a Means of Extending the Ministry Beyond the Span of One Individual

According to Mark 3:13-19, Jesus selected twelve from the larger group of His followers to form a group that would eventually extend the work He was inaugurating during His earthly ministry. According to this passage, Jesus chose them that they might be with Him, to learn from Him, and to then go out and extend His work. From the gospel narratives to the book of Acts, we see that this original group of twelve apostles were appointed, trained, anointed by the Holy Spirit, and sent out to extend the work of our Lord, starting in Jerusalem, in all Judea, in Samaria, and to the end of the earth (Acts 1:8).

For today's leaders, ministry teams are one of the most fruitful means of accomplishing the work of ministry. It is through teams that leaders accomplish the work of ministry. Teams provide support to leaders, teams serve as an effective way of organizing other leaders and workers, and teams extend the work of the ministry beyond the reach of an individual leader.

Leaders Need Others to Meet the Needs of the People They Serve

As ministries and churches grow and become more diverse in terms of membership and needs, the greater the potential for conflict over resources and priorities. One of the ministries of the church of Jerusalem was the daily distribution of food/meals for widows. According to Acts 6, the ranks of disciples were beginning to swell to such numbers that apparently needs of some members of the congregation were not being met. In fact, the Greek-speaking Jews complained to the Hebrew leaders that the Greek-speaking widows were being neglected. The apostles, or leaders of the Jerusalem church, model what we now know to be a Church Full of Leaders' principle. The apostles did not abandon their ministry tasks, but they sought out leaders from among the ranks

to place over this ministry; they sought out seven leaders who, according to Acts 6:3, were to have a "good reputation, [be] full of the Holy Spirit and wisdom" to "appoint over this business." Notice a few leadership principles.

First, the apostles sought multiple leaders; we might now see this as a New Testament church leadership team. Second, the apostles sought to place leaders over this work from within the congregation, reinforcing for us that leaders exist at many levels of a congregation and need to be identified, developed, appointed, and supported. Finally, the leaders they sought out had to have core leadership qualities—they had to be of good reputation (or of good standing and well respected), full of the Holy Spirit, and wisdom.

Today, the more demands are placed on our ministries and churches, the more we need to identify or develop qualified leaders to help lead the ministries.

Defining A Team

A team is a group of three or more people working together to achieve a common purpose that could not be achieved by the individual members working alone.

The Iceberg of Team Dynamics

Having explored the biblical basis of ministry teams, we still need to understand the dynamics and functioning of teams. There are two levels of teams that help ministry leaders work effectively with and on teams: the purpose level and the process level. Teams are much like icebergs:

Only a small portion of the mass of an iceberg is visible above the water level (estimates range from 10-14 percent); while the bulk of the iceberg is hidden below the surface. Team dynamics function much the same way.

Teams have a stated purpose that, if clear to all, serves as a means of visibly bringing the team together. We call this **Level 1 Team Dynamics.** Sometimes the purpose is articulated in a formal statement; at other times it entails the meeting agenda and specific goals set forth for the team to accomplish. The clearer these Level 1 activities, the more likely team members will be on the same page with respect to the team's purpose. Yet there are process issues that are less visible and dependent upon team members' understanding and ability to complete team tasks and work together interpersonally.

Level 2 Team Dynamics entail the task-process dimensions of the team: what people do on the team to accomplish the purpose. These activities may include holding meetings, making decisions, and conducting research.

Yet beneath the surface, there are also interpersonal processes that operate, sometimes latently. These processes include how people interact to accomplish the purposes of the team. Skills necessary to lead these processes, such as handling conflict and running effective meetings, are provided throughout this section of the Church Full of Leaders handbook.

As you see, leaders in a Church Full of Leaders must become adept at leading ministry teams and navigating the complex waters of team dynamics.

Challenges of Leading a Ministry Team in a Church Full of Leaders

Many leaders are accustomed to individual efforts, but individual effort is limited. God did not create us to work and serve alone.

Many leaders feel the one who has the most to say is the one with the most power. Consequently, leaders have to listen closely to the voices of people on the team and create a process by which every team member's voice can be heard. Leaders must believe that everyone on the team brings value and has something to add.

Team decision making most often takes longer, so leaders must be patient and have solid team processes and protocols. Team processes are more complex and require finer-tuned leadership skills.

Types of Ministry Teams

In churches in which leaders want to maintain vibrant ministries, yet are not large enough to hire staff for major ministry functions, identifying and forming leadership teams around those ministry functions is key. Looking at our Transformative Ministries chart, a few key leadership teams come to mind:

Evangelism and Outreach. This team is charged with leading and coordinating the major outreach of the church.

Worship. There are many possibilities for teams within the worship function of the church, from an operations team that works with the pastor on synching all aspects of the worship services to the praise and worship team to the liturgical praise/worship team. These are specialized teams devoted to ministering together to lead the congregation in worship.

In addition, there are operational teams that are not necessarily liturgical in nature but serve to keep the "operations" of the service flowing. These include the security team, greeters, ushers, and audio-visual, to name a few. These teams often comprise sub-teams of people assigned to serve together on a given Sunday, such as the first Sunday crew. Leading these types of teams require leaders who are adept at organizing multiple teams of servants, training members on the ministry processes, scheduling, and following up.

Education. There are many possibilities for team within the Education functions. Sunday school is typically one of the larger ministries of the church, organized according to age group (adults, young adults, teens, school-aged children, and toddlers/infants). The teams that are active for Sunday school may include a leadership team that provides guidance for the Sunday school, oversees curriculum decisions, provides/coordinates teacher development, oversees the teaching team (or team of teachers for each age group) and provides guidance and systems for recruiting and tracking new students. Other Christian education teams may include the leadership development team, the church retreat team, or the Bible school/ministry school leadership team.

Fellowship. As we saw in earlier chapters, fellowship ministries are those ministries formed around demographic groups of the church, including men, women, married couples, singles, and so on. These ministries are usually very programmatic in nature, and leadership teams for these ministries need to be structured in such a way as to facilitate and enhance ministering to the members alongside the pastoral ministry. Ministry activities may include workshops on topics germane to that group, social activities that facilitate fellowship, or even outreach to people in the community.

Care and Support. Care ministries are those that facilitate the care of the congregation. A care team may be the leadership team that organizes, trains, and dispatches care ministers to congregants in need. The care leadership team may consist of a combination of clergy and lay people who feel called to pray with members in various stages of needing care and support—from those in bereavement, to those in hospitals and nursing homes, to those "shut in" at home.

Administrative/Operations. Many churches are not in position to hire full-time administrative staff for overseeing office functions, tracking and managing the finances of the church, coordinating the communications strategy of the church, or managing the maintaining of the facilities. Administrative teams would comprise members who give their time to administer the functions and processes of ministry.

As we see, churches, regardless of the size, are complex organisms in need of being organized. Employing leadership teams in every key area helps with the organizing and leading of the various ministries and provides an infrastructure able to support growth. Ministry is not done by isolated individuals but through teams of people working together to accomplish a common mission.

Formal Ministry Roles

In a Church Full of Leaders, ministry teams comprise leaders who serve the team in a variety of capacities as each exercises his or her gifts and carry out the ministry work of the team. Such a team is not a traditional group with one leader who directs the activities of the group. Instead, teams in a Church Full of Leaders can best be described as a team of leaders, with each leader on the team carrying out a particular role and function for the overall success of the team. Following are examples of formal roles that may be needed for programmatic and operations types of teams.

Team Leader: The team leader is the person to whom God has given responsibility for facilitating the vision for ministry and the person that has been entrusted to rally other leaders together to fulfill the ministry vision. In a Church Full of Leaders, the team leader serves as a leader of leaders and helps to facilitate ministry processes. This person is responsible for leading the team toward the vision, for developing the strategic plan for the ministry, organizing meetings, communicating with the pastor(s)/pastoral staff, coordinating the implementation of programs, and ensuring the financial integrity of the ministry.

Program Team Leader: This person leads the development of major programs for the ministry team if the team's purpose is programmatic. Program teams include affinity group ministries and educational ministries and entail development of ministry programs for the edification, education, and enlightening on congregational members. The team leader may serve this program team role, or as the church and ministry grows, may identify a separate program team lead.

Operations Leader: For teams that are more operational in nature, e.g., they serve or operate on a regular basis to support worship or other processes of the church, an operations lead trains and schedules volunteers to serve in the ministry. In most churches, these ministries include the ushers, greeters, security, and audio-visual ministries. In small to medium-sized churches, it also includes maintenance and administrative teams.

Administrative Leader: The ministry team, whether programmatic or operations, will need a lead for administrative functions of the ministry. For instance, for programmatic teams, the administrative lead and his or her team handle things such as maintaining the ministry membership database and mailing list, and registering and tracking attendance for ministry programs. For operational teams, this administrative lead

will maintain the membership database as well as coordinate and track orientation and training schedules for new team members.

Communication Leader: The ministry team will need to develop a communication strategy to publicize ministry vision and programs. The communication coordinator is the leadership team member who directs the public communication of the ministry team. This role includes working with key departments (i.e., graphic arts department, newsletter department and announcements) within the church or with approved vendors to communicate adequately and appropriately messages concerning the ministry's functions.

Ministry Engagement Leader: The ministry engagement leader, or volunteer coordinator, is the ministry team member that coordinates the overall "volunteer" needs of the ministry. He or she ensures that each program has an adequate number of people to ensure success by coordinating with the church's ministry engagement organization. The ministry engagement leader and his or her sub-team members maintain and support the volunteer pool for ongoing program implementation.

Other team roles may be designated depending on the function of the ministry team and the size and complexity of the ministry.

Team Process

The most effective teams develop and perfect their team process—how they work together. Norms, protocols, and procedures are process elements that enable a team to operate effectively. Most ministry teams develop norms for operating. These norms are not always explicitly stated … they just emerge over time as the accepted practices and patterns of the team. Team members just abide by the norms without thinking or challenging why they do what they do. Norms such as promptness and courteous communication, for instance, are helpful to the team. On the other hand, tardiness, lack of accountability, unresolved conflicts, and poor follow through are just a few of the norms that keep a ministry team from operating effectively, efficiently, and in excellence.

Maturing teams must explicitly examine the norms that have developed to determine their appropriateness for their teams' functioning. The intent of developing clear operating procedures is not to institute rigid legalistic rules within the team but to help the team establish boundaries that support the established roles and provide parameters within which team members can operate. With clear boundaries and norms, team members know what to expect and can depend upon one another to perform within the guidelines.

In the chart above are examples of norms that have helped teams operate successfully. Leaders in your church will want to take the time to review and refine their own list of norms.

Team Dimension	Effective Norm
Notifications about meetings	Regular meeting dates are set in advance and team members are reminded about meetings at least 1 week in advance.
Communication in meetings	Meeting leader provides an agenda and solicits input from all team members; meeting notes and action plans are distributed to the team members.
Assignment of tasks/distribution of ministry activities	Tasks are shared among team members and team members are expected to follow through and complete their tasks by deadlines set.
Attendance at ministry events	Leadership Team members support ministry programs sponsored by the ministry and assist in areas as needed.
Spiritual activities	Team meetings start with prayer and a devotional reflection activity. In addition, team leaders periodically set times of collective prayer on behalf of the ministry.

Stages of Team Development

Ministry teams, like people, develop and mature—probably because ministry teams consist of people who are developing and maturing.

Over the past 30 to 40 years, many studies have shown that there are distinct stages of growth or development that teams experience. Not all teams go through all stages and become high performers. Furthermore, different teams take different amounts of time to go through each stage. This module will describe a five-stage model of team development, using labels derived from Tuckman's Model.[1]

Moving from a collection of individuals to a highly functioning team

Stage 1: Forming

As leaders, when we first form our teams, as much as we have prayed about team member selection and as familiar as we may be with individuals on the team, bringing different people together to serve on a ministry team entails forming a new entity that can take on a life of its own. We are bringing together people who we (and they) believe—or at least hope—are called to a particular ministry and have gifts and skills to offer for the ministry. Yet each person who joins the team is at a different stage of spiritual growth, each brings her or his unique personality to the team, and each brings his or her history of interpersonal

interactions to the team. Each hears from God differently. Each develops and follows plans differently. Surely the apostle Paul in teaching about the diversity of gifts in the body had ministry teams in mind!

In a Church Full of Leaders, as the church grows, many of the leaders selected to serve on leadership teams may be new to serving on ministry teams. Consequently, when we bring our new team members together, these team members are generally excited to serve; in fact, they will most likely be honored to serve. Those that have served in other capacities before will still be excited about this new endeavor.

Team leaders will want to lay a good foundation for their teams by being very intentional in the Forming stage, keeping the following points in mind:

- Team members generally have positive expectations about the ministry.
- Team members are eager to start on the work of the ministry.
- Team members look to the ministry leader for direction.
- Team members want clarity on mission, purpose, objectives, "Why are we here?"
- Team members begin to sort out "Why am I here?"
- The team does not accomplish much during this stage.

Leader Suggestions: Remind leaders not to be in too much of a hurry to get right down to work. Encourage them to take time to get to know team members and build trust among team members. Team leaders set the tone for their teams by being timely and reliable, following good meeting techniques (such as reviewing the team's mission, using an agenda, and sending out meeting notes) and following through on commitments. Team leaders must encourage forthright talk on the team and must not stand for harmful communication such as backbiting or gossip. Leaders will want to help team members connect and fit, and feel that they can trust the team leader and other members. At this stage the leader and members focus on the call to serve, carrying out the mission of the ministry and getting to know one another.

Stage 2: Storming

Storming is the stage of team development in which conflict begins to surface. As we will see in the next chapter, conflict is not necessarily a bad thing. It is inevitable when humans with distinct personalities and diverse backgrounds work together but it does not have to be destructive. Although conflict may arise at any of the stages, it is expected in this early stage of the team's development, as team members are still getting to know each other, still learning styles and work patterns, still testing boundaries as to what is accepted and not acceptable behavior.

No matter how clear the leader sets the initial charge to the team as to why they were chosen to serve, at some point members will interpret that mission through their own filters and may propose ministry ideas that are not in sync with how another leadership team member interprets the mission. No matter how much a team leader prays for guidance on task assignments, a team member may "drop the ball" and create a "hiccup" for the team's operations. What is needed is for the team to mature, for team members to build more trust with one another, and for team members to translate their individual implicit values into explicit shared values that guide how they handle issues. Remember, conflict in and of itself is not bad. How a team weathers the storm when it comes will determine how the team continues to develop or stagnate.

Team leaders will want to provide unifying processes that help put team members on one accord without squashing the diversity of opinions and ideas that surface on a ministry team. The goal is unity not uniformity. Keep the following in mind for successfully navigating teams through this stage:

- Conflict arises within the team as people attempt to clarify goals, roles, rules, and direction. Take time to clarify.
- Factions may appear as members attempt to build support for their own ideas. Take time to stress unifying themes.
- Team skills increase gradually. Acknowledge those skills.
- Task accomplishments increase slowly. Take your time—don't rush through this stage.
- It is critical that the team prayerfully, but effectively, deal with the conflict. Take time to pray.

Leader Suggestions: Deal with conflict openly and expeditiously in a manner consistent with Jesus' model of walking in love, even when dealing with conflict. Encourage leaders to be consistent with all team members and reinforce the value of all members to the team. Remind leaders to do a "process check" when conflict arises, and take the time to work through disagreements. Help leaders to make healthy conflict resolution techniques the norm for their ministries, such as reminding members that all discussions of the conflict must be held at that place and time, not in "meetings after the meeting," or in "one-on one" gripe sessions over the phone. Those ways of handling conflict are not healthy for the team.

Check the desired outcomes of team members. Go around the room and ask each person what he or she wants from the ministry team. Post the answers to a chart to get personal agendas on the table and give team members an opportunity to express their concerns, which may be at the heart of the conflict. Use personal/team style inventories such as the Myers-Briggs Type indicator or

the DISC assessment to help team members learn about the different styles on the team and learn to effectively leverage these style differences.

Stage 3: Norming

As the team continues to mature, things will begin to "gel." Team members learn what works and doesn't work for each of them and for the team overall. The team starts accomplishing some of its goals and realizing what it takes to be successful together.

At this stage, the team leader and leadership team members have developed a team structure or roles and responsibilities that work. They have figured out meeting schedules and communication norms that work.

At this stage, team leaders may note the following:

- Productivity—what the team accomplishes together steadily rises.
- Team member expectations have begun to fall in line with reality.
- Structure has become clear.
- The team is making progress toward team goals.
- Relationships continue to be built and are becoming settled.
- Cohesion begins to develop.
- Accepted behavior is clarified.
- The limits to individual roles are tested.

Leader Suggestions: Take time to set or reset ground rules and team operating procedures. Communicate more rather than less. Affirm positive accomplishments of the team. Take time to review goals and make sure individual goals are integrated with the overall team purpose. At this stage, make sure roles are clear. Keep the team focused on the next milestone.

Stage 4: Performing

After much prayer and growing together, the team starts accomplishing its goals. Be they programmatic or operational, with the help of the Lord and godly leadership, the team is making it happen.

At this stage, team leaders will note the following:

- The team begins to gel and coalesce even more.
- The team members are positive and excited about their accomplishments.
- The team's productivity and accomplishments are high.
- Team members feel good about being a part of the team and the team identity is strong.

- The confidence of team members has increased.
- Members are able to work autonomously and then come back together to report progress on task accomplishments to the team.
- Team members begin to assume leadership for various aspects of the team.

Leader Suggestion: Continue to meet, pray and connect. Allow other team members to share leadership. At this stage it is crucial that a ministry program plan has been developed and is being followed. Review that plan and accomplishments of milestones at each meeting. And by all means, celebrate those accomplishments and continue to hold functions in which team members spend time with each other, continuing to fellowship and build relationship.

Stage 5: Transforming

Just as transformation occurs for individuals when their thinking and mind-sets are changed and affect how they behave in the world, teams transform as team members rethink who they are and how they do what they do in light of their mission and the needs of the people they serve. At this mature stage, team members can reflect on the team and what they've accomplished and maturely assess what has worked and what has not worked, and make course adjustments for the good of the people for whom they minister. It is at this stage that new members may be invited onto the team and other team members may request to leave the team. In any event, this stage represents an opportunity for a powerful shift in the team. At this stage, Team Leaders will note the following:

- Serving on ministry teams provides opportunities for transformation, not only of the people served by the ministry, but also of the ministry team members and of the ministry itself. Celebrate the growth.
- At this stage, team members recognize how they have been changed by other members of the team, and how they have come to depend on the Lord more by virtue of working through difficult team processes. Celebrate the growth.
- At this stage, the team members can also acknowledge the need for new ways of doing things. Celebrate the growth.

Leader Suggestions: Take time to reflect, renew, and celebrate. Use a program or process evaluation to review your team's ways of operating. Consider using a ministry survey to get input from ministry members. Take time to pray about the future direction of the team—where to stay on course and where to make adjustments.

Here are some **closing tips** for building an effective ministry team:

- **Provide Purpose.** As you and other leaders structure ministry teams for your Church Full of Leaders, provide each team with a clear purpose. Make sure that the ministry team has a clear mandate and serves a purpose within the church. Then develop processes by which the ministry purpose is shared with new leaders and members of the team.

- **Build Trust.** Trust is the glue that holds any team together. As team members work through early stages of team development, and learn to trust the leader and one another, the team grows in cohesiveness and is strengthened to forthrightly address conflicts that might otherwise shipwreck the team.

- **Clarify Roles.** Team members must understand the distinct reason they are on the team and the role they will play in fulfilling the team's purpose. No purpose, lack of role clarity, and role overload cause members to become frustrated with the team. God created and placed us in the body of Christ for each of us to play a role and be connected to one another. Ministry teams provide a means of connecting members to one another through service and support.

- **Garner Commitment.** Team membership must be turned into member engagement. In other words, team members must be connected to each other and to the work and held accountable for their tasks. As people are clear on the purpose of the team, given valuable roles to fulfill, and see the path and ultimately the results of their work, the more they will grow in commitment.

- **Implement Plans.** Teams come together to do, to perform, and to implement. After team members have grown together, increased in their ability to work together, they must be unleashed to implement the plans they have prayerfully pulled together.

- **Strive for High Performance.** Provide teams with expectations of excellence. Give them guidelines and watch them live up to your highest expectations.

- **Renew Strength.** Give team members opportunity to debrief and review their performance. Give them time to celebrate their successes and give them time to recharge and rebuild before the next major team ministry project.

Chapter 16—Reflection

1. What additional biblical passage can you think of to support team ministry?

2. What have you observed about team dynamics in your church? In your board meetings? In your ministry/pastoral staff meetings? In your administrative staff team meetings?

3. In the space below, describe and list the ministry team structure of your church. Now that you have read this chapter, what roles may be missing in your structure? How clearly have you shared this ministry structure with your leaders?

Let's face it. No matter how well organized or spiritually mature leaders of a congregation are, there is bound to be times when leaders disagree on purpose, procedures, or just plain clash due to personality differences. Conflict in and of itself is not a sign of an immature leader, but how that leader handles conflict is a sign of his or her maturity and effectiveness.

Though there are various types of conflict that leaders must be acquainted with, and they must develop skills for resolving conflict without isolating or harming others, leaders must first and foremost discern the very nature of conflict itself.

Conflict can occur between people. Conflict can be defined as a difference in opinion, purpose, goals, or expectations that frustrate the realization of goals or desires. A leader may engage in interpersonal conflict in which two or more people disagree over incompatible goals, differences of opinion, or unclear expectations. Unfortunately, leaders can also have conflict over overly invested egos.

Conflict can occur on teams. Leaders may also experience conflicts within their ministry teams. These occur when the leader experiences interpersonal conflict with a member or members of the team. Yet team conflicts may also center around missed objectives by the team, problems the team can't solve, or unclear goals. These issues affect an entire team and must be resolved at the team level.

Conflict can occur at the institutional level. Leaders may also experience institutional or structural conflicts. These result from incompatible mission—a team is not aligned with the church or the church's mission is unclear, and individual leaders go about getting things done using very individualized ways, often to the detriment of other ministries. The methods of leaders or groups within an organization or institution can lead to conflict for senior leaders. For instance, when there are limited resources at the institutional level, ministry teams may find themselves vying for budget dollars to underwrite their programs to find space to hold their ministry events.

The methods for resolving and handling each of these types of conflict must be in line with the level of conflict. Interpersonal conflicts, for instance, need interpersonal resolution. Team conflicts need team resolutions and institutional conflicts need organizational resolutions. Too often a leader tries to resolve a conflict between two people in front of the entire team. Not only is the resolution aimed at the wrong level, but also it stirs up more anxiety on the team, thus creating conflict at the team level.

The levels of conflict are interconnected. Clearly, interpersonal conflict affects the team and team conflict affects the organization or institution. Leaders must become adept at paying attention to how conflict ripples through their team or organization and identify the systemic conflicts. How does our set-up, or organization, create conditions for conflict? What policies or structures reinforce conflict conditions? What practices do we engage in that create conditions for partisanship, favoritism, or exclusion?

Spiritual Dynamics of Conflict

To be effective methods for resolving conflict, they must be used in the hands of mature, spiritually discerning leaders. Too often leaders who are spiritually immature and rife with inner conflict open themselves to the enemy to become the purveyor or stirrers of ongoing conflict.

Let's take a look at broader scriptural principles around conflict. Let's look for a moment at the church at Corinth, a church founded by the apostle Paul but rife with conflict. The members were riddled in partisan church politics identifying with specific ministry leaders to the exclusion of others. Some felt they were the disciples of Paul, others of Apollos, and still others of Peter (1 Corinthians 1:12). Perhaps these were the apostles or leaders who God used to bring them to salvation, and out of allegiance they aligned with those specific teachers. But Paul taught them that their loyalty to an earthly leader, no matter how gifted, was misplaced. As disciples, they were first and foremost followers of Jesus Christ. In this church were also those who disrespectfully challenged authority.

It's similar to what occurs in our contemporary churches When we have strong and charismatic leaders, members choose their favorite teacher or pastor and can't seem to tolerate other teachers in the congregation. Paul's message to the Corinthians was to remind them of their need to grow and mature from attitudes such as those reflected in partisanship (1 Corinthians 3:4). Mature leaders didn't take sides with other leaders; they sided with truth.

Yet Paul also reminded this church that there was another source of conflict that they needed to be aware of. God desires to have churches reflect His love and people who reflect His love in the earth realm. The enemy comes to kill, steal, and destroy, and he is subtle and sneaky in the ways he comes to disrupt the work of God and distract the people of God. When you find yourself in a lot of conflict, strife, and argumentation, consider whether or not the enemy and his imps are somewhere wreaking havoc trying to disrupt the program of God.

The enemy uses or capitalizes upon the various elements of conflict to heighten dissension and alienate individuals. When a ministry experiences pervasive, ongoing conflict, ministry leaders must discern the spiritual root of such conflict. Such deep-seated spiritual conflict manifests as follows:

- **Persistent Blaming/Accusing/Condemnation.** According to Revelation 12:10, Satan is the accuser of the brethren "who accused them before our God day and night." Blaming and accusations are not devices that help people grow, nor do they draw people closer together. Blaming and accusations divide and shame. When ministry leaders and team members blame one another and accuse one another, they are using tactics that reinforce the enemy's agenda and not God's. Mature leaders provide feedback and correct behavior without developing or reinforcing a culture of blame that sometimes results from the leader's pride and inability to reflect on his or her own role in the ministry issues. Dietrich Bonhoeffer, in writing to pastors of the underground church in Nazi Germany, admonished pastors never to complain about members to God.

- **Lies, Falsehoods, Deception, Untruths, Cover-Ups.** Deception and all forms of lying engenders and fuels division and conflict. A mature, strong ministry must be founded upon the truth of God's Word. According to John 8:44, Jesus reminded the conflictual Pharisees, "You are of your father the devil…He abode not in the truth, because there is no truth in him, When he speaks a lie, he speaks of his own; for he is a liar, and the father of it."

- **Sinful Anger and Other Works of the Flesh.** Paul taught the church in Ephesus many things that were crucial to building up the body of Christ. He stressed for members of the church to not let anger become a tool of the devil (Ephesians 4:26-27). Sinful anger and all works of the flesh give the enemy place or opportunity to infiltrate and wreak havoc.

- **Spiritual Laxness.** Time and time again, the apostle Paul wrote, "we are not ignorant" or "I would not have you to be ignorant" (Romans 1:13. Romans 11:25; 1 Corinthians 10:1, 1 Corinthians 12:1. 2 Corinthians 1:8). Paul's aim in teaching and writing to the churches he founded was that they would know God's will for the church. That knowledge was based in a spiritual and experiential understanding. Peter made it even more clear, as he wrote to Christians in the first century. He wrote, "Be sober, be vigilant, because your adversary the devil, as a roaring lion, walks about, seeking whom he may devour" (1 Peter 5:8). That roaring lion seeks to isolate and attack and will prey upon those who are not vigilant or paying attention.

- **Envy and Strife.** James gives us profound insight into how envy and strife can wreak havoc in ministry. He declares that "where envy and strife are, there is confusion and every evil work" (James 3:15). He teaches

that envy and strife emanate from fleshly wisdom—from people who think and act according to their own wisdom. But this type of wisdom is not from God and does not build up the work of God. Instead it is self-serving and leads to diabolic division (James 3:15).

- **Unforgiveness.** There was the conflict of values in the Corinthian church such that a man had to be reprimanded and disciplined because he engaged in immoral behavior. Yet after a time, Paul admonished the leaders to forgive him and comfort him, lest he would be swallowed up with extreme sorrow and the church leaders fall victim of one of Satan's devices. Paul was teaching them and us today that unforgiveness festers in our hearts and fuels conflict, dissent, disengagement, and destruction. Too often ministry leaders flounder because they have become bitter through unforgiveness. They can't minister the love of Christ because they've not opened their hearts to be healed of that root of unforgiveness. It is the enemy's strategy, not God's, to keep us from forgiving and letting off the hook those who have offended or hurt us.

Spiritual conflict must be resolved through spiritual means (2 Corinthians 10:4-5). So before we move into skills for resolving conflict, we must help every leader understand that the root of resolving conflict starts in our hearts. We must remain humble and open to the work of the Holy Spirit to mature us and do the inner work necessary to not be a conduit of conflict that stems from selfish, fleshly motives that are then exacerbated by the enemy of the work of God.

Peacemaker Ministries® is dedicated to helping people resolve conflict and make peace in biblical, God-honoring ways. The intent of this section is not to replicate what they do but to help you understand an overall approach to resolving conflict—whether its interpersonal, team, or organizational. At the heart of this approach is a biblical framework. Additional resources can be found at PeaceMaker.net.

The 4 Gs of Conflict Resolution[1]

Glorify God (Matthew 5:1). Devote yourself to making sure God gets glory out of all that is happening. Whether we are on the receiving end of conflict or we are the ones who have offended another, when we move forward with the aim of glorifying God, it elevates our motives to those that are God honoring and not self-serving.

Get the Log Out of Your Own Eye (Matthew 7:3-5). Before you start blaming or criticizing another person, look within your own soul and consider what you may have done to add to, or fuel, this conflict through your:

- Attitudes
- Words
- Actions

Gently Restore (Matthew 18:15-20). After looking up and looking within, there comes a time when you will need to go to your brother or sister to help him or her understand what he or she did to offend you.

- Use a gracious tone of voice and conciliatory gestures when giving this feedback
- Be objective in your feedback—make it about the issue and do not personalize it about the person
- Use the Bible carefully—don't overuse or misuse Scripture to beat the other person over the head

Go and Be Reconciled (Matthew 5:23, 24). Be willing to let go and be reconciled to your brother or sister.

- Forgive
- Let it go
- Move on

Now that we have defined the levels of conflict, explored the spiritual roots of conflict, and provided a tool for approaching another person as a brother or sister, let's discuss a strategy for actually approaching that person.

Handling Conflict Dialogue Strategy for Ministry Leaders

As ministry leaders, you will be required to handle conflicts that arise in your ministry that are not necessarily anchored in offense. Differences arise in ministry teams due to conflicting opinions and perspectives or from varying experiences. Conflicts that arise in ministry can sometimes be emotionally charged, and the tendency may be to get defensive and discuss the issue in deeply personal ways. The key to resolving these conflict issues is to engage the other person in dialogue so that deeper insights and eventual solutions may arise. The following is a strategy for you to use when team members or others come to you about a conflict in the ministry.

Dialogue is a distinct form of communication about which we'll say more in the next chapter on communication. For now, let's look at a strategy based on the mutuality that arises from a dialogic approach to conflict.

Create Space for Dialogue

- **Start with prayer.** Use the tips of the 4G methods to ask God for guidance, to seek to glorify God, and to examine your own heart.
- **Carve out the appropriate time and place to have the dialogue.** Whether giving feedback, starting a dialogue to resolve conflict, or assisting ministry members in resolving conflict, make sure you have adequate time to work through the issue; and make sure you have a private place.
- **Respect the other person as a sister or brother in Christ.** See the other person as deeply loved by God as you are and who is growing and in need of grace, as you are
- **Suspend your assumptions about what you think the conflict is or what the causes are.** Too often we bring those assumptions to the "table" and our preconceived notions hinder our ability to listen openly to the issues.
- **Listen graciously and non-defensively.** To do this, you must make the 4Gs of the previous section an ongoing practice.

Discover the Issues of the Situation

- Inquire into the behaviors and actions that led to the clash. Distinguish between intent and impact. You first and foremost want to assume positive intent on the other person's part—that is an act of grace. In actuality, you may never know the person's real intent; you can only speak to the impact his or her behaviors had on you, the team, or the organization.
- Shift your perspective to try to understand where the other person is coming from, how the clash made him or her feel, what may have prompted his or her actions, and so on. Your ability to empathize will go a long way to helping to keep the relationship intact long after the actual problem is resolved.
- Share your understanding of the situation and its impact. As honestly, sincerely, and objectively as possible, share your understanding of the situation in behavioral terms. Refrain from making inference about motives, judgments about the person. Don't allow your emotional or cultural filters to shade the way you describe what happened. Be honest about the impact on you—how the incident or situation made you feel. Don't blame. Instead take ownership for your own feelings, attitudes, behaviors, and reactions.

Reconcile the Differences

- In addressing conflicts in ministry, you want to resolve the issue and maintain relationship. To do so, you must advocate for resolutions or outcomes that are fair to all parties involved. The parties in a conflict may not see the issue the same, but to continue to work together and for both

parties to grow from the conflict, they must commit to reconciliation. Reconciliation of the difference will entail truthfully speaking to each party's role in the conflict, and the parties being able to ask for and offer forgiveness. In other words, be willing to apologize for any of your actions that led to or fueled the conflict or misunderstanding. Be willing to forgive. Being able to forgive quickly, without harboring grudges, or holding on to offenses, is a sign of spiritual maturity.

- After the parties have reconciled, it is wise to have the parties agree to mutual problem-solving to address underlying issues that may have led to the conflict or to avoid a repeat of the conflict.

- Finally, always commit to follow through. Whether you are one of the parties in conflict or a ministry leader helping team members work through conflict, follow up within a reasonable time frame to ensure the parties are moving forward together.

Chapter 17–Reflection

1. As a leader, what types of conflicts do you experience most often in your ministry?

   Interpersonal

   Team

   Institutional

2. Now with insights from this chapter, how might you approach those conflicts differently?

3. Take a moment to reflect on how your institutional structures and policies may be creating conflict conditions. How are your ministries set up or organized that may create conditions for conflict? What policies or structures reinforce conflict conditions? What practices do ministry leaders engage in that create conditions for partisanship, favoritism, or exclusion?

Communication is the process for sharing messages and conveying meaning to one or more people. Consequently, communication occurs at many levels in the church and is instrumental in creating the culture of each church. Through communication of the rituals and practices of a given church, the church is creating and cultivating its distinctive character. In a Church Full of Leaders, communication is critical to helping unite leaders, to putting leaders on one accord, and to perpetuating the life of the church.

Spiritual communication

Because church is both organism and organization, church communication is multidimensional, but at its core, it is spiritual. At its most basic, prayer is a type of communication between God and the people of God. The heart of preaching and teaching is to convey spiritual messages that uplift the heart and spirits of people, as well as inform and strengthen their minds. The aim of spiritual communication is to edify and build up the people of God at the very core of their beings, such that their lives reflect the One who called them and saved them.

Member communication entails the ways we communicate interpersonally with one another, member to member. Yet member communication invokes many of the lessons from Scripture on how we ought to speak with one another (e.g., in love and with grace) and entails reminding us of our tone, attitude, and perspective in interacting with one another.

Messages that church leaders, particularly pastors, have to share with the congregation through preaching and teaching are critical to the church. The preaching and teaching style of ministers, the structure of sermons, and the audio-visual and technological supports are all informed by technical communication. But we must never forget this communication is intended to touch the heart.

Organizational Communication

As stated previously, the church is an organism—a dynamic, growing entity made of ever-growing beings. Yet the church is also an organization—a structured association of members who worship, learn, and serve together. In natural sciences we are told every organism organizes itself so the dynamic living church is organized to fulfill its function. Organizational communication then is the communication strategies and tactics that facilitate the work of ministry. It is both informative and transformative. It is through communication that ministry leaders inform members of church operations, ministry events, protocols, etc. Yet is also through various types of communication that ministry leaders proclaim the gospel, provide care and support, and build and strengthen relationships within the body of Christ.

Group/Team Communication

Because the work of ministry is done by ministry teams within the church, understanding how we best communicate in groups, as well as how we communicate from team to team, is important. Communicating messages and information so that ministry teams share the church's vision, are aligned to the mission, can coordinate the work of ministry, and share limited resources is all facilitated through communication.

Mediated Communication

Mediated communication addresses how media helps the church convey its messages to members, surrounding communities, or the public at large. Borrowing from marketing communication, mediated communication helps to establish the brand of the church—the reputation and image a church conveys to the outside world. Yet mediated communication also helps church leaders reinforce and strengthen messages to and among members.

Before we delve into the specifics of each of these types of communication, let's start with God and examine how He communicates with us. In so doing, we gain insight into what ought to be the very heart, or spirit, of all of our communication in the church.

God's Communication with Us

Communication of Character

God is Sovereign. God is in charge. God is in control. Theologians say God is transcendent yet at the same time immanent. The old saints used to say, "God sits high and looks low." The only way we, as humans, even come to know or grasp God is by God's own self-revelation, which is God's way of communicating His very nature or character to us. God reveals His Love (1 John 4:8), His righteousness (Romans 1:17), His immutability (Hebrews 6:17), His power (1 Corinthians 1:24; 1 Peter 1:5), His wisdom (1 Corinthians 2:7; Ephesians 3:10), His consistency (Malachi 3:6), His plans and purposes (1 Corinthians 2:10), and even His wrath (Romans 1:18) to us and, thus, communicates His very nature to us. In like manner, as ministry leaders called and chosen by God, when we communicate with people, our communication will reveal our nature or character. What we say out of our mouths will reflect and reveal what is truly in our hearts—for out of the abundance of the heart the mouth speaks (Matthew 12:34). Be sure you continually do the work of the heart to ensure your words are authentic and genuine. There is no place in ministry for deceit or manipulation.

Communication of Love

The story of the Bible is the story of God's love relationship with humankind. Our story is intricately interwoven into this story. The meta-narrative of God is about the love God has for people. And in many ways across the ages, God has revealed and demonstrated His love for humans with the ultimate expression of that love being embodied in Jesus Christ. "For God so loved the world, He gave His only begotten son, that whosoever believes in Him should have everlasting life" (John 3:16). Clearly and in human terms, God communicated His love to us by giving and coming where we are. In so doing, God reveals His heart to us and models for us that we, as ministry leaders, must communicate in such as way as to convey God's heart to the people we lead. What we do and what we say must always be motivated by love—our love for God and for God's people.

Communication of Presence

Words are the building blocks of communication. It was through words that God created the heavens and the earth. God said, and it was what He said. It is significant then that God revealed to John that "[i]n the beginning was the Word, the Word was with God and the Word was God …and the Word became flesh" (John 1:1; 14). The Word walked among us, lived among us—was present with humans. The very mind and thoughts of God became flesh, embodied in Jesus. Likewise, our words become flesh when they become embodied in us—in our actions. Our words become flesh as we offer people we serve and serve with the gift of presence—as we walk alongside them and serve with them side-by-side, we are communicating that we are "in this boat together!" The ministry of presence cannot be over-emphasized.

The Heart of Member Communication

The Bible provides principles for us to follow in our communication with each other:

Speak the truth in love

But, speaking the truth in love, may grow up in all things into Him who is the head —Christ, Ephesians 4:15, NKJV

Instead, speaking the truth in love, we will grow to become in every respect the mature body of him who is the head, that is, Christ. Ephesians 4:15, NIV
When speaking to the church at Ephesus, Paul emphasized the ministry to and in the body of Christ. When admonishing about growth of the body and the members of the body, he declared we must speak the truth in love in order to grow and grow up.

God-pleasing communication
May the words of my mouth and the meditation of my heart be pleasing in your sight, O LORD, my Rock and my Redeemer. Psalm 19:14, NIV
Too many people underestimate the power of words. The leader's aim must be to make sure his or her words are pleasing to God.

Consistency of our words
But above all, my brethren, do not swear, either by heaven or by earth or with any other oath. But let your "Yes," be "Yes," and your "No," "No," lest you fall into judgment. James 5:12, NKJV

Leaders create confusion when what they say does not line up with what they do. When giving guidance and instruction to staff members, ministry team leaders, or the broad congregation, let people know what you want from them. Make your expectations known, so people do not have to guess. Before implementing new projects or introducing change to the church, let people know what is coming. Then let them know how you will get through the change together. As a leader, if you change your mind, let people know. Don't let them have to guess what you are doing or what you want them to do.

Listening
Understand this, my dear brothers and sisters! Let every person be quick to listen, slow to speak, slow to anger. James 1:19, NET

In an extroverted, media-saturated world, listening is not always modeled or valued. In ministry, leaders must listen. Leaders listen for the Spirit to reveal. Leaders listen to members. Listening intently to another person lets that person know he or she is important to you and what he or she has to say is valued.

Giving and receiving feedback—speak the truth in love
Listen to advice and accept instruction, that you may gain wisdom in the future. Proverbs 19:20, ESV

Giving and receiving feedback is a critical communication skill, especially for ministry leaders. Yet it seems that giving feedback to ministry members is one of the more difficult tasks in ministry leadership, and it is even more difficult for ministry leaders to receive feedback. Yet feedback is necessary for effective team functioning and for personal growth. In a Church Full of Leaders, leaders must be mature enough to give and receive feedback to one another.

Communicate with grace

Let your speech always be with grace, seasoned with salt, that you may know how you ought to answer each one. Colossians 4:6, NKJV

Let your conversation be gracious and attractive so that you will have the right response for everyone. Colossians 4:6, NLT

We are to communicate graciously with our words, our tone, our gestures, and our facial expressions. These all convey the deeper meaning behind our words.

Developing a Communication Strategy

A communication strategy is an integrated, systematic plan that articulates how your church will communicate. The strategy delineates the purposes, methods, and audiences for multiple levels of communication in the church. It will take into consideration the core spiritual nature of church communication, organizational communication (church-wide communication) both in and outside the church, group-level communication (e.g., ministry teams and auxiliaries), member communication, and mediated communication.

Conducting a Communication Survey

As you continue to develop your communication strategy, consider conducting a communication survey—either congregation wide or in specific ministries. The communication survey will help you determine the communication needs and preferences of the congregation.

Consider using the survey to also collect updated communication information from the congregants such as their current e-mail, cell phone number, and social media handles. Make it easy for members to take the survey. Inform the congregation that the pastor and leadership team are interested in enhancing church-wide communication and want to learn the congregation's preferences and needs. Let them know the time period in which the survey will be conducted. Make it easy for members to take the survey.

For your current membership that is in your e-mail database, e-mail a survey to them and provide reminders. For members not connected to e-mail, set up survey stations throughout the church that will allow members to stop by and take the survey before or after services. Make sure your team is well-organized to collect and track surveys.

Sample Communication Survey

Name:_____ e-mail:_____

Cell Phone: _____

Twitter Handle:_____ Facebook Name: _____

Demographics

❏Teens	❏20s	❏30s	❏40s	❏50s	❏60s	❏70s	❏80+
❏Single	❏Married	❏Widowed	❏Divorced				

1. How do you prefer to receive communication/information about church programs?

Sunday announcements	
Church bulletins	
Church Web site	
E-mail reminders	
Word of mouth	
Calling church office for automated messages about events	

2. Which of the following do you currently use and/or follow?

E-mail	❏Yes ❏No
Texting	❏Yes ❏No
Facebook	❏Yes ❏No
Twitter	❏Yes ❏No
Instagram	❏Yes ❏No
Blogs	❏Yes ❏No
YouTube	❏Yes ❏No
Other	❏Yes ❏No

3.   Which of the following would you be willing to start if taught?

E-mail	❑Yes ❑No
Texting	❑Yes ❑No
Facebook	❑Yes ❑No
Twitter	❑Yes ❑No
Instagram	❑Yes ❑No
Blogs	❑Yes ❑No
YouTube	❑Yes ❑No
Other	❑Yes ❑No

4. In the space below, please share any additional information you would like for us to know about your communication preferences.

Compiling and Using Survey Results

The survey data will help church leaders develop their communication strategy. The results can be compiled in such a way to give you a sense of communication preferences by age, gender, or any other demographic category you choose to collect (e.g., ministry).

Because you asked and members took the time to respond, you definitely want to act upon the survey by sharing the compiled results with the congregation and informing them of how their responses are helping to shape the communication strategy. Keep the congregation abreast as you enhance and build the components of your communication strategy.

Organizing the Way You Think About Organizational Communication

Organizational communication for churches entails the communication that entails the messages that go out on behalf of the entire church, or those messages aimed at touching the entire congregation (sometimes called church-wide communication).

A simple scheme to organize organizational communication for churches is external (those messages targeted at people outside of the local church, internal (those messages targeting members), or dual (those messages targeting people in and outside of the local church).

External—to build the brand, image or connection to/with external stakeholders. Purpose: to inform and to attract	Dual—to connect members, prospective members to the church, spreading the preached Word, teaching sessions Purpose: inform and transform (evangelistic, edification)	Internal—to build community and connect us to one another Purpose: to inform and transform (instruction and care)

External communication—the messages the pastor and church project to the "outside world," to external stakeholders, to surrounding communities

- LED Signs that brand the church and announce regular and special services to people within the community
- Broadcast messages of services and teaching sessions
- Church Web site to which people can go to learn about the church
- Newspaper articles or press releases that inform people about church events
- Social media (Facebook, Twitter, etc.) that inform and connect people to the church
- Mass mailers that invite people to the church
- Radio/TV announcements of events that inform people of church events

Internal communication—the messages pastor, church leaders, and members convey to one another

- Mass e-mails that inform members of church events (as the church continues to grow, use an e-mail blast service such as Constant Contact)
- Mass texting that informs members of church events, especially events that are time sensitive (as the church grows, use a texting service)
- Print bulletins that provide information on upcoming events
- Sunday morning announcements (live or mediated) that provide information of upcoming events
- Communication boards or posters (including the signage of the church) that inform of upcoming events but also celebrate occasions of ministries
- Information center or kiosk that provides a place for members and visitors to get information

- Web site to which members can go to download sermons, review calendar of events, etc.
- Phone trees or robo calls that disseminate information to members
- Conference calls used for prayer calls or connecting calls for specific ministries or all members
- Newsletters that provide members with updates, upcoming events, and church-interest stories; these could be hard copy or electronic
- Church-branded apps that allow ministry leaders to push sermon notes, announcements, etc.

Dual–the methods used to reinforce the teachings of the church, to disseminate the teachings and messages of the church beyond the walls of the church

- CDs/DVDs and podcasts of preached or taught messages to reinforce messages for members and introduce teaching to non-members
- Web site used to attract members and non-members via blog or posted messages
- Live streaming of services
- Radio/TV publication of messages to disseminate the preached and taught Word
- Social media to connect members and nonmembers to the church

Ministry Team Communication

Communication About the Ministry Team

Ministry pages on the Web site aim to inform visitors to your Web site about the ministries of your church. Descriptions about the ministry on the Web site and other church materials should be purposeful and clear. Ministry teams can use the same format given in chapter five on developing the mission statement to write ministry descriptions. Whereas the church has a mission, ministry teams have a purpose. Ultimately, the purpose of ministry teams is to help fulfill the mission of the church.

Communication Within Ministries

Each ministry within the church is led by a leadership team. Team leaders must have a system of communication in which team members are notified of meetings, meeting minutes are shared, and other updates are provided to the team leaders.

At the same time, communication for ministry teams aims to help ministry leaders communicate with people who serve in or are otherwise affiliated

with their ministry. This communication would include sharing information with ministry members, informing members of upcoming ministry services or events, and encouraging ministry members during challenging times such as bereavement or illness.

Mediated Communication

Mediated communication entails all the ways media and technology are used to facilitate communication in and out of the church.

Broadcasts

Many smaller, but growing churches do not have a budget for airing their church services on the broadcast venues. The strategy must be to develop a plan in which, as the church grows, media becomes a priority to provide the church with the exposure it needs to both spread the message of the gospel and to attract people to the church. Until the TV ministry is fully developed for broadcast on regional or national networks, following are some suggestions for ministry broadcasts for the small to medium-sized church:

- Local cable stations
- Live streaming using free or low-cost streaming services
- Providing DVDs of prior services to visitors
- Sharing podcasts of sermons and teachings
- Uploading video to the church's Web site
- Creating a YouTube page and uploading portions of services/sermons, or providing a link to the YouTube videos from the Web site. Other video-sharing services include Vimeo or Facebook

Social media

We live in a media-saturated world. With 24-hour cable news outlets reporting news around the clock, and with social media such as Twitter, Facebook, LinkedIn, Instagram, and other sites providing venues for us to disseminate our messages at the touch of a finger, we are a communication-heavy culture. Social media can be a great resource or tool for churches.

In the broadest sense, the aim of social media is to inform and connect people. It can be used to inspire people with daily inspirational messages. It can be used to enable people to connect to your church or pastor who might not ordinarily connect. It provides leaders with a vehicle for announcing services, especially special services.

Stats. When one billion people are on Facebook and half a billion people are on Twitter alone, why wouldn't a church want to takes its message to where people are.[1] Many of these social media platforms are extremely easy to use and to get started on. In fact, if the pastor or pastoral leaders are uninformed or

a little reticent, most likely there are people within your congregation already using these platforms. Enlist them, and not the team, to build your social media strategy. There are Web designers who will ensure the social media pages are congruent with the church's Web site. Ask around in your network to identify a great Web designer who also does social media to design and/or integrate your sites. If all else fails, post a request on your personal Facebook page!

Connecting the Congregation

Once you have your Web site and social media platforms designed and up and running, the first people you want to connect with your sites are the members of the congregation. Develop a communication plan that informs them about the new mediated communication platforms, invites them to connect (or follow), and encourages them to spread the word to their social networks. However, there may be members who are not yet using any social media platforms but may want to learn. Develop a brief workshop for these members to teach them about social media, how to get and stay connected, and use it as a tool for connecting others to their church.

Summary

Communication connects. Communication coordinates. Communication is vital to a Church Full of Leaders. The church leader that communicates strategically and intentionally connects members to the church vision and mission. Church leaders use communication to coordinate ministries and members. Used well communication both informs and transforms, both attracts and connects. Used well and sensitively, leaders use communication to help build community and create a culture of inclusion and love. A Glossary of Technology Apps that can be helpful for churches is found in the appendix.

Chapter 18—Reflection

1. Think about your leadership style for a moment. What does it communicate to others about you, your commitment to or vision for ministry, and your care for others?

2. Non-verbal communication such as facial expression, tone and posture communicate just as much as words. Have you ever been told by someone that you were conveying an emotion you thought you were concealing or was contrary to how you were truly feeling?

3. How comprehensive is your ministry communication strategy, and how aware are all your leaders of this strategy?

Meetings, meetings, meetings—the mundane but necessary activities in church leadership. Think of the worst meeting you ever attended. A few may come to mind. Most likely, those meetings dragged on for hours, as the meeting organizer or leader attempted to cover too many topics in one sitting. Or perhaps those meetings were poorly organized with no clear sense of purpose.

Now think of the best meetings you have participated in. Not only were the qualities of those meetings the polar opposite of the worst meetings, but something special was created among team members—a sense of unity and anticipation of next steps. These types of meetings are not only effective, but they are also essential to engaging and equipping members in a Church Full of Leaders.

What is a meeting?

A meeting is a structured gathering or coming together of people with a common purpose to solve a problem, collaborate on an issue, develop ideas, or resolve issues. These days meetings can be held face-to-face, via conference call, or video conference. Effective meetings are vital to ministry leaders and members alike, and few people have time or patience to waste in ineffective meetings.

Why Meet?

Both the apostles and the elders met together to deliberate about this matter.
Acts 15:6, NET

The work of ministry is accomplished through people who come together for common purposes of praying, organizing, planning, programming, and/or fellowshipping. Meetings are the vehicles through which ministry leaders and members come together in structured ways.

Let's look briefly at a meeting that was held shortly after Jesus' ascension and departure from His apostles to identify four critical components to meetings. For ages believers have come together for structured communal prayer. In this case, one hundred and twenty disciples met in the upper room to pray and await the promised Holy Spirit. While there, they conducted the business of selecting a new apostle to replace Judas.

Participants

Then they returned to Jerusalem from the mount called Olivet, which is near Jerusalem, a Sabbath day's journey. And when they had entered, they went up into the upper room where they were staying: Peter, James, John, and Andrew; Philip and Thomas; Bartholomew and Matthew; James the son of Alphaeus and Simon the Zealot; and Judas the son of James. (Acts 1:12-13).

Preparation

These all continued with one accord in prayer and supplication, with the women and Mary the mother of Jesus, and with His brothers. (Acts 1:12-14, NKJV)

Purpose

And in those days Peter stood up in the midst of the disciples (altogether the number of names was about a hundred and twenty), and said, "Men and brethren, this Scripture had to be fulfilled, which the Holy Spirit spoke before by the mouth of David concerning Judas, who became a guide to those who arrested Jesus; for he was numbered with us and obtained a part in this ministry. (Acts 1:15-17, NKJV)

While waiting in that upper room, the apostles regrouped and selected a new apostle to replace Judas. It's interesting to note that they had a meeting leader who directed the meeting and at least one critical item of business. After connecting their mission to the prophetic words of Psalm 41:9 that another should take the office of the one who had betrayed the Lord, they proceeded to select a new apostle.

Process

Therefore, of these men who have accompanied us all the time that the Lord Jesus went in and out among us, beginning from the baptism of John to that day when He was taken up from us, one of these must become a witness with us of His resurrection." And they proposed two: Joseph called Barsabas, who was surnamed Justus, and Matthias. And they prayed and said, "You, O Lord, who know the hearts of all, show which of these two You have chosen to take part in this ministry and apostleship from which Judas by transgression fell, that he might go to his own place." And they cast their lots, and the lot fell on Matthias. And he was numbered with the eleven apostles. (Acts 1:21-26, NKJV)

- Peter laid out the criteria for selecting the new apostle.
- They proposed two candidates.
- They prayed.
- They cast lots to make the selection.

Now some people argue that the apostles should have prayed and not held a business meeting, for we never hear from Matthias as an apostle after this incident. Perhaps that is true. What this passage shows us though is the structure of meetings from the early church. And the same features—participants,

preparation, purpose, process—can be used to plan, run, and evaluate our meetings today.

Meeting Management—A Three-Part Process

A helpful model for understanding the structure of meetings is the three-phase model. Every meeting can be related to three distinct phases—before, during, and after.

Before You Meet

There are a series of questions every ministry leader should ask prior to calling a meeting of team or ministry members.

- Is it necessary to bring people together?
- What is the purpose of our coming together?
- What is the best format for our coming together? Face to face, conference call or video conference?

When planning your team meetings, keep these points in mind:

1. Effective meetings are carefully planned with a clear concept of what the meeting is for and the goals you want to meet.
2. The meeting is enhanced when team members contribute something to and derive something from the meeting. Plan the meeting with the ministry team members or participants in mind.
3. An agenda serves as a road map for the meeting—it lays out the steps to get the outcomes of the meeting accomplished. Prepare an agenda in advance to help keep the meeting on track and enhance team members' ability to participate. Distribute the agenda in advance of the meeting if team members have topics to cover on the agenda.
4. Don't overcrowd your agenda, cramming too many topics into the allotted time.
5. Give team members plenty of time to schedule and prepare for the meeting.

During the Meeting

A well-planned meeting practically runs itself! The meeting leader must be mindful of time and facilitate keeping the meeting on track. In some ministry teams, members will veer off track with conversation on issues not related to the task at hand. It is the responsibility of all participants to help keep the meeting on track, but the formal responsibility for this task will fall to the meeting leader. During the meeting make sure to:

1. Use the agenda as a road map.
2. Facilitate the meeting process, encouraging members to participate but not prolong discussions not related to the meeting purpose.
3. Pay attention to team-member dynamics and how members are relating to one another, especially in less-mature teams.
4. Make sure actions and key decisions are recorded.

After the Meeting

Meeting minutes or notes provide a means for participants to recall what was decided or acted upon in the meeting. They provide a record of key decisions and action steps. They help remind team members of commitments made and next steps for the team in reaching its overall goals and objectives. Ideally, minutes should be distributed to team members in a reasonable time frame after the meeting, especially if there are action steps to be taken on the part of the team members. Meeting minutes can be e-mailed to members. Some meeting recorders will take notes on their smartphones and can e-mail minutes or notes directly from their electronic devices.

Meeting Technology

A number of technologies exist to help leaders conduct great meetings. Some are free, which will help the budgets of smaller churches yet allow leaders of these churches to hold efficient and effective meetings using the latest in Web-based technology. Do your homework for the technology that best meets your church's need. See the appendix for Glossary of Technology Apps.

Meeting Checklist

Phase One: Planning the Meeting
❏ Clearly define the purpose of the meeting
❏ Determine the necessary participants
❏ Determine whether conference lines or video conferencing is needed
❏ Develop topics/issues to be addressed
❏ Define the desired outcomes of the meeting
❏ Define the meeting roles
❏ Decide on room arrangements
❏ Develop and distribute the agenda

Phase Two: Conducting the Meeting
❏ Start meeting on time
❏ Clarify roles (meeting leader; recorder)
❏ Follow agenda

❑ Develop follow-up action plan
❑ Evaluate the meeting

Phase Three: Following Through with Meeting Items

❑ Develop and distribute meeting minutes
❑ Plan for next meeting

Closing tips

- Use the three-phase model to prepare and run your meetings.

- Meetings are necessary for leading effective ministry, but meetings do not need to be a waste of time for members.

- Schedule meetings ahead of time at regular intervals, such as monthly on the first Saturdays or second Wednesdays so team members can include meetings in their calendar in advance.

- Send reminders (or have reminders sent) for meetings.

- Model healthy meeting behaviors by starting and ending on time.

- Don't structure fun out the meeting. Continue to build camaraderie during meetings.

Chapter 19—Reflection

1. How would you rate the quality of your current meetings?

2. What are the current church or organizational norms around meetings?

3. Are those norms helpful or harmful to productive meetings? How might you change the norms if they are not helpful?

A Final Word: You Hold the Key

Developing church leaders is an awesome task, and the *Church Full of Leaders* process helps you approach leadership development scripturally, systematically, and strategically. The context and needs of ministry are complex and no one person can adequately lead the church by himself or herself. Untapped talent is sitting in your church, and the *Church Full of Leaders* process provides you with a means for developing a plan to engage more members into the ministries of your church.

Church leadership is not elitist or reserved for people with specialized education alone. Church leadership is not about a position, but it is a process of transformation to which all believers are called to participate in some form or fashion. Building a *Church Full of Leaders could be the start of something phenomenal in your church. You hold the key to unlock the secrets to effective leadership development and unleash the leadership potential of your church.

This manual was written with you in mind. Perhaps you are a new pastor and desire tools to help you in your new role. You will soon learn you need leaders to do the work of ministry with you. Perhaps you are a pastor of a church in transition. You will need tools to align your leaders and make sure they are on the same page as you. Perhaps you are a pastor of a church who desires to leverage more of the spiritual and human potential sitting in the pews.

My prayer is that you will embrace the ideas found in this manual and use the tools to build your own Church Full of Leaders. As you grow personally, you will desire more growth for your congregation. As your congregation grows, you will need to enlist more leaders into the process to accomplish the God-given purposes for your church.

Church Full of Leaders Visioning Team

The Church Full of Leaders visioning team is the group of people committed to praying and working with the pastor to develop the leadership vision for the church. The members of this team will need to thoughtfully study the Church Full of Leaders manual together and commit to participate in a leadership visioning retreat. Members of the visioning team could include current members of the board, leaders of ministries, and a representation of the congregation.

Church Full of Leaders Leadership Development Team

The Church Full of Leaders leadership development team shepherds the church through the Church Full of Leaders process. The members of this team consist of a cross section of current leaders of the church. They are responsible for helping to plan, monitor, and implement the process under the guidance of the pastor, director of ministries, or leadership facilitator. This group will also be responsible for shepherding the Church Full of Leaders process through the ministries they lead, as well as reviewing and helping to customize the Church Full of Leaders training to more closely meet the needs of their church.

Church Full of Leaders Trainer/Training Team

Once the Church Full of Leaders training is customized, a training team must be identified. This team will be responsible for delivering the information in the Church Full of Leaders training modules to current leaders, upcoming leaders, and potential leaders. The training team is often a subset of the Church Full of Leaders development team.

Church Full of Leaders Training Coordinator

The Church Full of Leaders training coordinator is a member of the Church Full of Leaders training team and sets the training calendar, schedules the appropriate space and venue for the training, ensures the training site is properly set up and arranged, arranges for the appropriate audiovisual equipment, assures the proper amount of training materials are ordered and arrive on time, as well as develops the appropriate forms and systems to keep track of attendees.

Church Full of Leaders Communications Coordinator

The Church Full of Leaders communications coordinator is a member of the Church Full of Leaders training team and develops a communication plan for notifying the current leaders of the training schedule and requirements. The communications coordinator develops a comprehensive communication plan for each phase of the Church Full of Leaders training that includes flyers, posters, bulletin announcements, and pulpit announcements.

There are numerous spiritual gift inventories and descriptions of the gifts. Some listings are based on a particular denominational perspective, while others are very broad and inclusive of a wide array of gifts shared with humans through Scripture. Following is a listing of spiritual gifts taken from the New Testament church leaders (Paul and Peter) as given in Romans, 1 Corinthians, Ephesians, and 1 Peter. Included in this listing are brief descriptions of each spiritual gift including the scriptural reference for the gift, the Greek word, and its literal translation, followed by a phrase that operationally defines the gift for application.

Administration—1 Corinthians 12:28 Gk: *Kubernesis* — steersperson, governor.

- The Spirit-given capacity and desire to serve God by organizing and managing the resources of the church, thus promoting the effective and efficient execution of ministry.

Apostle—Ephesians 4:11-12; Gk: *Apostolos* — a messenger on a mission; one sent out on behalf of another, as a delegate or representative for a mission.

- The Spirit-given capacity for pioneering and advancing the gospel in previously unreached areas, as well as providing authoritative leadership and accountability for those ministries, churches and leaders.

Discernment—1 Corinthians 12:10; Gk: *Diakrisis*—distinguishing, discerning, judging; the discerning of spirits.

- The Spirit-given capacity to judge and distinguish whether behavior that is claimed to be from God is in actuality truly from God, the flesh, or of the enemy.

Exhortation (Encouragement)—Romans 12:8; Gk: *Parakaleo* — to address or speak to in such a way as to give comfort, entreaty or instruction. To console, encourage, and strengthen by consolation, to comfort.

- The Spirit-given capacity and desire to serve God by admonishing, inspiring, motivating, encouraging, and strengthening others in their Christian walk.

Evangelism—Ephesians 4:11-14; Gk: *Euaggelistes* — a bringer of good tidings; an evangelist.

- The Spirit-given capacity to share the gospel of Jesus Christ with such conviction that people become disciples and followers of Christ. Though all believers are given the great commission to share the gospel and make disciples, some are particularly gifted by the Spirit to evangelize and share the gospel in ways that compel unbelievers to make a decision to receive Christ.

Faith—1 Corinthians 12:9 Gk: *Pistis* — a firm conviction or belief respecting the things of God, generally with the idea of trust in God and His Word.

- The Spirit-given capacity to firmly believe God for that which seems impossible and to trust God's promises and purposes for His work and people. Though all believers are given a measure of faith, some have been endowed by the Spirit with such great faith to what is impossible in the natural realm.

Giving—Romans 12:8 Gk: *Metadidomi* – to impart, give, contribute.

- The Spirit-given capacity and desire to share generously and cheerfully of one's material resources in order to advance the work and ministry of God. Though every believer is compelled and commanded to be a steward of the resources of God, through their tithe and offering, the Holy Spirit endows some believers with supernatural capacity to give and share of their resources above and beyond to help and assist the work of ministry. These givers are often gifted to amass great treasure out of which they serve the Lord.

Healing—1 Corinthians 12:9,30 Gk: *Iama* — healing, remedy.

- The Spirit-given capacity to restore health to the sick.

Helps—1 Corinthians 12:28 Gk: *Antilempsis* — giving of one's time and means to assist in the Lord's work, in general; to "lend a hand" to the relief of the poor or other ministry tasks and assignments.

- The Spirit-given capacity and desire for doing practical and necessary tasks that support and meet others' needs. People with

the gift of helps often are found serving behind the scenes, being available to others in very practical and dependable ways.

Hospitality—1 Peter 2:9-10; Romans 12:9-13 Gk: *Philoxenos* — hospitable, generous to guests

- The Spirit-given capacity for graciously extending welcome and kindness to other people. The gifting to care for people by means of fellowship, food, shelter, and/or creating a safe, comfortable environment where others feel welcomed.

Knowledge/word of knowledge—1 Corinthians 12:8; Gk: *Gnosis*—knowledge, understanding, moral wisdom

- The Spirit-given capacity to understand and grasp divine revelation. It manifests in the ability to grasp facts that cannot be readily known.

Leadership—Romans 12:8 Gk: *Proistemi* — to lead, govern, or rule

- The Spirit-given ability to envision the will and purposes of God for the church or a ministry; an anointing for setting God-given goals and communicating these goals in such a way as to inspire others to willingly and harmoniously work together to accomplish the goals for God's purposes and glory.

Mercy—Romans 12:8 Gk: *Eleeo* – to have mercy on; to help one afflicted or seeking aid; to feel sympathy with the misery of others

- The Spirit-given ability to be sensitive to the pain, suffering or hardship of others, with the desire to compassionately act to help lessen the pain, suffering, or hardship.

Serving—Romans 12:7; I Peter 4:9-11. Gk: *Diakonia* — service

- The Spirit-given capacity and desire to serve by volunteering one's time and resources to assist in ministering to the needs of other people.

Prophecy—1 Corinthians 12:10, 28, Gk: *Propheteia* – a discourse emanating from divine inspiration and declaring the purposes of God, whether by reproving

and admonishing the wicked, or comforting the afflicted, or revealing things hidden, especially by foretelling future events.

- The Spirit-given ability to convey the mind and heart of God to the people of God through divine declarations.

Shepherding/Pastoring—Ephesians 4:11-14, Gk: *Poimen*—one who herds sheep, e.g. a shepherd

- The Spirit-given ability to care for and provide nurture to the people of God, specifically a group of believers who have committed themselves to said leader. It is the ability and desire to serve God by leading, equipping, and caring for a group of believers. A person with this gift may or may not be called to the office of the pastor but is specially endowed with the capacity to care for, nurture, and help develop members of the body of Christ.

Speaking—1 Peter 4:11; Gk: Laleo — to utter a voice; to speak; to use words in order to declare one's mind and disclose one's thoughts.

- The Spirit-given ability to convey a message by spoken word, so that numbers of listeners have full opportunity to understand and be inspired, informed, and/or instructed.

Teaching—1 Corinthians 12:28, Ephesians 4:11-14; Romans 12:7. Gk: *Didaskalos*—one who provides instruction concerning the things of God and the attendant duties of the people of God.

- The Spirit-given capacity and desire to serve God by making clear the truth of God's Word, especially as it relates to the overall well being of the body of Christ.

Wisdom—1 Corinthians 12:8; Gk: *Sophia* — the wisdom of God

- The Spirit-given capacity to grasp the mind of the Holy Spirit in such a way as to receive insight into the application of knowledge for specific situations and needs arising in the body of Christ.

Position Description Template—L1 Leader (Ministry Member)

POSITION TITLE: _____

REPORTS TO: _____(Small Group or Team Leader)

POSITION SUMMARY (Customize to your church)

The primary responsibility of a ministry team member is to lead designated projects or tasks for a ministry team or small group, follow through to completion of tasks or projects and provide updates or report of activities.

POSITION RESPONSIBILITIES (Customize to your church)
- Assists Small Group Leader with designated asks
- Provides updates on tasks to the small group/team leader
- Submits reports where applicable

COMPETENCIES (Customize to your church)
Maturing Spiritual Walk—demonstrates spiritual growth and qualities of a maturing leader
1. Consistently practices spiritual disciplines such as Bible reading and prayer
2. Consistently gives of his or her time, talent, and tithe
3. Maintains a biblical lifestyle and uses the Word to guide his or her choices
4. Attends and participates in corporate prayer, worship, and Bible study

Willingness to Assume Ministry Responsibility
1. Demonstrates faithfulness to ministry
2. Conveys interest, calling, or passion to the ministry
3. Follows ministry leadership

Shows Initiative in Ministry Responsibilities
1. Demonstrates creativity and innovation in tasks assigned
2. Follows through on tasks assigned
3. Follows up with other ministry members to complete tasks
4. Provides timely updates to ministry leaders and members

Organization—demonstrates the mastery of one or more organizational leadership skills

1. Serves effectively on a ministry team
2. Follows through on projects or tasks that are started
3. Consistently demonstrates promptness to meetings and other ministry activities
4. Able to organize agendas or lesson plans

Position Description Template—L2 Leader (Small Group/Team/Class Leader)

POSITION TITLE:_____

REPORTS TO:_____ (Ministry Leader)

POSITION SUMMARY (Customize to your church)
The primary responsibility of the small group/team leader is to lead a small group, ministry team, or class, facilitating member growth and connection to the church.

POSITION RESPONSIBILITIES (Customize to your church)
- Prepares lessons plans or program plans using the standard materials designated by the church
- Teaches Bible lessons based on standard materials and age-appropriate learning aids and facilitation techniques
- Regularly attends small group leadership meetings for curriculum or program review and/or staff development
- Tracks class attendance and provides reports to the ministry leader
- Follows up with absent members

COMPETENCIES (Customize to your church)
Communication—the ability to effectively convey ministry information and plans orally and in writing to a variety of constituents, including staff, ministry leaders, and volunteers
1. Effectively and clearly communicates the strategic and tactical objectives and plans to appropriate parties
2. Maintains a tracking system for tactical objectives/plans to limit miscommunication
3. Communicates with candor in a manner in which information can be received positively and with consistency across various functions of responsibility

Interpersonal Leadership—the ability to demonstrate interpersonal competence that builds trust and enhances interpersonal relationships in ministry
1. Listens well to others, non-defensively and with openness to hear the heart of issues
2. Maintains confidentiality
3. Communicates and conveys ideas and thoughts clearly
4. Gives and receives feedback
5. Resolves conflict biblically

Spiritual Leadership–demonstrates a commitment to spiritual growth and facilitating the spiritual growth of others; the ability to set the spiritual tone for the ministry and provide the type of leadership that inspires through consistent modeling of spiritual disciplines and practice, both public and private

1. Demonstrates Word-based faith and is faithful
2. Is sensitive and in tune with the Holy Spirit, as well as his or her own interior life
3. Lives out of a clear or (growing) sense of purpose
4. Exhibits godly character as evident in his or her attitudes and actions
5. Leads with and in love—demonstrates care and compassion toward others
6. Demonstrates unity
7. Lives a biblically defined holy life
8. Demonstrates wisdom in decision making

Ministry Proficiency or Gifting–demonstrates a proficiency or gifting in a specific area of ministry, such as teaching, audio-visual, food services, health education, and so on

1. Has skills in a specific administrative or ministry area
2. Demonstrates capable gifting for service, including helps
3. Demonstrates faithfulness in serving, using skills and gifts
4. Demonstrates willingness/initiative to serve, using skills and gifts

Maturing Spiritual Walk—demonstrates spiritual growth and qualities of a maturing leader

1. Consistently practices spiritual disciplines such as Bible reading and prayer
2. Consistently gives of his or her time, talent, and tithe
3. Maintains a biblical lifestyle and uses the Word to guide his or her choices
4. Attends and participates in corporate prayer, worship, and Bible study

Willingness to Assume Ministry Responsibility

1. Demonstrates faithfulness to ministry
2. Conveys interest, calling, or passion to the ministry
3. Follows ministry leadership

Shows Initiative in Ministry Responsibilities

1. Demonstrates creativity and innovation in tasks assigned
2. Follows through on tasks assigned
3. Follows up with other ministry members to complete tasks
4. Provides timely updates to ministry leaders and members

Organization–demonstrating the mastery of one or more organizational leadership skills

1. Serves effectively on a ministry team
2. Follows through on projects or tasks that are started
3. Consistently demonstrates promptness to meetings and other ministry activities

Position Description Template—L3 Leader (Ministry Leader)

POSITION TITLE: _____

REPORTS TO:_____ (Department Leader)

POSITION SUMMARY (Customize to your church)
The primary responsibility of the ministry leader is to lead the ministry and includes overseeing the various teams within the ministry. The ministry leader is a leader of leaders and works closely with his or her ministry leadership team to provide direction for the ministry and carry out the ministry's programs, classes, or ministry events.

POSITION RESPONSIBILITIES (Customize to your church)
- Provides oversight for ministry operations, ensuring quality biblical instruction where appropriate, timely and effective ministry management, member tracking, and offering collection/budget tracking
- Oversees the review, selection, ordering, securing, and distribution of curricula or other pertinent materials to meet objectives of the ministry
- Works closely with ministry team leads
- Provides facilitation and instructor development for small group/team/class leads
- Identifies, recruits, and develops new small group/team or class leads

COMPETENCIES (Customize to your church)
Program Leadership—the ability to execute or implement ministry programs, projects, or interventions that align with the pastor's vision; demonstrates the ability to follow a framework for a new or existing ministry or educational program, project, or service
1. Has experience, knowledge, and familiarity with Bible, spiritual formation, and/or Christian education development principles and practices, and demonstrates the ability to translate those principles into effective curricula and ministry programs
2. Develops or contributes toward the improvement of programs that go beyond the status quo and moves the ministry team to a new level
3. Has the ability to engage appropriate people and gain buy-in to ministry programs
4. Maintains and tracks ministry budget

Teamwork—the ability to build and effectively lead ministry teams to accomplish ministry and program objectives
1. Partners effectively with other departments to implement ministry programs effectively
2. Partners effectively with ministry leaders to develop and implement ministry programs successfully
3. Follows and assists ministry leadership with administrative processes

Meeting Leadership—the ability to run effective meetings to disseminate information to the department or ministry team, as well as bring the team together to maintain cohesiveness and build unity around common goals
1. Effectively plans meetings and notifies department of meeting objectives in advance
2. Effectively uses meeting tools such as agendas and minutes to maintain departmental communication
3. Effectively utilizes the resources of other departmental meetings to hold productive and fruitful meetings

Communication—the ability to effectively convey ministry information and plans orally and in writing to a variety of constituents, including staff, ministry leaders, and volunteers
1. Effectively and clearly communicates the strategic and tactical objectives and plans to appropriate parties
2. Maintains a tracking system for tactical objectives/plans to limit miscommunication
3. Communicates with candor in a manner in which information can be received positively and with consistency across various functions of responsibility

Interpersonal Leadership—the ability to demonstrate interpersonal competence that builds trust and enhances interpersonal relationships in ministry
1. Listens well to others, non-defensively and with openness to hear the heart of issues
2. Maintains confidentiality
3. Communicates and conveys ideas and thoughts clearly
4. Gives and receives feedback
5. Resolves conflict biblically

Spiritual Leadership—demonstrates a commitment to spiritual growth and facilitating the spiritual growth of others; the ability to set the spiritual tone for the ministry and provide the type of leadership that inspires through consistent modeling of spiritual disciplines and practice, both public and private

1. Demonstrates Word-based faith and is faithful
2. Is sensitive and in tune with the Holy Spirit, as well as his or her own interior life
3. Lives out of a clear or (growing) sense of purpose
4. Exhibits godly character as evident in his or her attitudes and actions
5. Leads with and in love—demonstrates care and compassion toward others
6. Demonstrates unity
7. Lives a biblically defined holy life
8. Demonstrates wisdom in decision making

Ministry Proficiency or Gifting–demonstrates a proficiency or gifting in a specific area of ministry, such as teaching, audio-visual, food services, health education, and so on

1. Has skills in a specific administrative or ministry area
2. Demonstrates capable gifting for service, including helps
3. Demonstrates faithfulness in serving, using skills and gifts
4. Demonstrates willingness/initiative to serve, using skills and gifts

Maturing Spiritual Walk—demonstrates spiritual growth and qualities of a maturing leader

1. Consistently practices spiritual disciplines, such as Bible reading and prayer
2. Consistently gives of his or her time, talent, and tithe
3. Maintains a biblical lifestyle and uses the Word to guide his or her choices
4. Attends and participates in corporate prayer, worship, and Bible study

Willingness to Assume Ministry Responsibility

1. Demonstrates faithfulness to ministry
2. Conveys interest, calling, or passion to the ministry
3. Follows ministry leadership

Shows Initiative in Ministry Responsibilities

1. Demonstrates creativity and innovation in tasks assigned
2. Follows through on tasks assigned
3. Follows up with other ministry members to complete tasks
4. Provides timely updates to ministry leaders and members

Organization–demonstrates the mastery of one or more organizational leadership skills

1. Serves effectively on a ministry team
2. Follows through on projects or tasks that are started
3. Consistently demonstrates promptness to meetings and other ministry activities

Position Description Template—L4 (Department Leader)

POSITION TITLE: _____

REPORTS TO:_____(Pastoral Staff Member)

POSITION SUMMARY (Customize to your church)
The primary responsibility of the department leader is to lead the ministry department, which includes multiple ministries within the church. The director will oversee the development ministry program strategies, special ministry processes that develop the ministry leaders in the department.

POSITION RESPONSIBILITIES (Customize to your church)
- Provides programmatic and development support to congregation-wide ministry programs and processes
- Oversees the review and selection of curricula to meet objectives of the department
- Oversees ministry programs leaders
- Leads one or more new congregational formation processes
- Develops strategies for the management of ministry teams
- Provides facilitation and instructor development for small group/team and program leads

COMPETENCIES (Customize to your church)
Organizational Leadership—the ability to build and effectively lead multiple ministry teams to accomplish departmental objectives; able to develop both ministry programmatic objectives and organizational/operational objectives, educational programs, projects, or interventions that align with the pastor's vision; helps to move the congregation foward.
1. Demonstrates the ability to systematically develop and articulate a framework for a new or existing program, project, or process
2. Has the ability to engage appropriate people and gain buy-in to ministry strategy
3. Partners effectively with other ministry departments to implement ministry programs effectively
4. Follows and assists ministry leadership with administrative processes
5. Develops and manages departmental budget

Program Leadership—the ability to execute or implement ministry programs, projects, or interventions that align with the pastor's vision; demonstrates the ability to follow a framework for a new or existing ministry or educational

program, project, or service

1. Has experience, knowledge, and familiarity with Bible, spiritual formation and/or Christian education development principles and practices, and demonstrates the ability to translate those principles into effective curricula and ministry programs
2. Develops or contributes toward the improvement of programs that go beyond the status quo and moves the ministry team to a new level
3. Has the ability to engage appropriate people and gain buy-in to ministry programs

Teamwork—the ability to build and effectively lead ministry teams to accomplish ministry and program objectives

1. Partners effectively with other departments to implement ministry programs effectively
2. Partners effectively with ministry leaders to develop and implement ministry programs successfully
3. Follows and assists ministry leadership with administrative processes

Meeting Leadership—the ability to run effective meetings to disseminate information to the department or ministry team, as well as bring the team together to maintain cohesiveness and build unity around common goals

1. Effectively plans meetings and notifies department of meeting objectives in advance
2. Effectively uses meeting tools such as agendas and minutes to maintain departmental communication
3. Effectively utilizes the resources of other departmental meetings to hold productive and fruitful meetings

Communication—the ability to effectively convey ministry information and plans orally and in writing to a variety of constituents, including staff, ministry leaders, and volunteers

1. Effectively and clearly communicates the strategic and tactical objectives and plans to appropriate parties
2. Maintains a tracking system for tactical objectives/plans to limit miscommunication
3. Communicates with candor in a manner in which information can be received positively and with consistency across various functions of responsibility

Interpersonal Leadership—the ability to demonstrate interpersonal competence that builds trust and enhances interpersonal relationships in ministry

1. Listens well to others, non-defensively and with openness to hear the

heart of issues
2. Maintains confidentiality
3. Communicates and conveys ideas and thoughts clearly
4. Gives and receives feedback
5. Resolves conflict biblically

Spiritual Leadership–demonstrates a commitment to spiritual growth and facilitating the spiritual growth of others; the ability to set the spiritual tone for the ministry and provide the type of leadership that inspires through consistent modeling of spiritual disciplines and practice, both public and private
1. Demonstrates Word-based faith and is faithful
2. Is sensitive and in tune with the Holy Spirit, as well as his or her own interior life
3. Lives out of a clear or growing sense of purpose
4. Exhibits godly character as evident in his or her attitudes and actions
5. Leads with and in love—demonstrates care and compassion toward others
6. Demonstrates unity
7. Lives a biblically defined holy life
8. Demonstrates wisdom in decision making

Ministry Proficiency or Gifting–demonstrates a proficiency or gifting in a specific area of ministry, such as teaching, audio-visual, food services, health education, and so on
1. Has skills in a specific administrative or ministry area
2. Demonstrates capable gifting for service, including helps
3. Demonstrates faithfulness in serving, using skills and gifts
4. Demonstrates willingness/initiative to serve, using skills and gifts

Maturing Spiritual Walk—demonstrates spiritual growth and qualities of a maturing leader.
1. Consistently practices spiritual disciplines, such as Bible reading and prayer
2. Consistently giving of his or her time, talent, and tithe
3. Maintains a biblical lifestyle and uses the Word to guide his or her choices
4. Attends and participates in corporate prayer, worship, and Bible study

Willingness to Assume Ministry Responsibility
1. Demonstrates faithfulness to ministry

2. Conveys interest, calling, or passion to the ministry
3. Follows ministry leadership

Shows Initiative in Ministry Responsibilities
1. Demonstrates creativity and innovation in tasks assigned
2. Follows through on tasks assigned
3. Follows up with other ministry members to complete tasks
4. Provides timely updates to ministry leaders and members

Organization–demonstrates the mastery of one or more organizational leadership skills
1. Serves effectively on a ministry team
2. Follows through on projects or tasks that are started
3. Consistently demonstrates promptness to meetings and other ministry activities

POSITION TITLE:_____

REPORTS TO:_____(Senior Pastor or Governing Board)

POSITION SUMMARY (Customize to your church)
The pastoral leader provides direction and leadership to the church, including facilitating and overseeing the ministry processes, developing new ministries, and developing the ministry leaders of the church; oversees ministry departments and assists with pastoral care, preaching, and teaching.

POSITION RESPONSIBILITIES (Customize to your church)
- Works closely with other pastors or governing board to help cascade pastoral vision throughout the congregation; helps launch new ministry initiatives; and develops and monitors processes that ensure ministry programs align with the vision and church mission
- Develops and implements leadership development processes and programs for the ministry leaders of the church, including providing facilitation support to designated ministries
- Helps provide training and tools for church staff and to aid in the facilitation and leadership development for designated ministry leaders
- Oversees pastoral-care functions
- Assists senior pastor with preaching and teaching

COMPETENCIES (Customize to your church)
Strategic development—the ability to develop ministry programs, projects, or interventions that align with the pastor's vision; helps to move the congregation toward the pastoral vision and/or innovatively meets the needs of specific groups within the church. Strategic development also includes the development of departmental leaders, ministry leaders, and team leaders
1. Demonstrates the ability to systematically develop and articulate a framework for a new or existing ministry program, project or service.
2. Has experience, knowledge and familiarity with Bible, spiritual formation, pastoral leadership, and/or leadership development principles and practices, and demonstrates the ability to translate those principles into effective ministry programs
3. Develops or contributes toward the development of innovative programs that go beyond the status quo and moves the church toward the vision
4. Has the ability to engage appropriate people and gain buy-in to ministry strategies

Pastoral Leadership–the ability to lead a church or a major function of a church by casting vision, and providing oversight to the spiritual and administrative processes of the entire church and its ministries

1. Demonstrates the ability to systematically develop and articulate a framework for a new or existing ministry program, project, or service
2. Has experience, knowledge, and familiarity with Bible, spiritual formation, pastoral leadership, and/or leadership development principles and practices, and demonstrates the ability to translate those principles into effective ministry
3. Develops or contributes toward the development of innovative programs that go beyond the status quo and moves the church toward the vision
4. Has the ability to engage appropriate people and gain buy-in to ministry strategies

Organizational Leadership—the ability to build and effectively lead multiple ministry teams to accomplish the departmental objectives; able to develop both ministry programmatic objectives and organizational/operational objectives, educational programs, projects, or interventions that align with the pastor's vision; helps to move the congregation foward

1. Demonstrates the ability to systematically develop and articulate a framework for a new or existing program, project, or process
2. Has the ability to engage appropriate people and gain buy-in to ministry strategy
3. Partners effectively with other ministry departments to implement ministry programs effectively
4. Follows and assists ministry leadership with administrative processes
5. Develops and manages departmental budget

Program Leadership—the ability to execute or implement ministry programs, projects or interventions that align with the pastor's vision; demonstrates the ability to follow a framework for a new or existing ministry or educational program, project, or service

1. Has experience, knowledge, and familiarity with Bible, spiritual formation and/or Christian education development principles and practices, and demonstrates the ability to translate those principles into effective curricula and ministry programs
2. Develops or contributes toward the improvement of programs that go beyond the status quo and moves the ministry team to a new level
3. Has the ability to engage appropriate people and gain buy-in to ministry programs

Teamwork—the ability to build and effectively lead ministry teams to accomplish ministry and program objectives

1. Partners effectively with other departments to implement ministry programs effectively
2. Partners effectively with ministry leaders to develop and implement ministry programs successfully
3. Follows and assists ministry leadership with administrative processes

Meeting Leadership—the ability to run effective meetings to disseminate information to the department or ministry team, as well as bring the team together to maintain cohesiveness and build unity around common goals

1. Effectively plans meetings and notifies department of meeting objectives in advance
2. Effectively uses meeting tools such as agendas and minutes to maintain departmental communication
3. Effectively utilizes the resources of other departmental meetings to hold productive and fruitful meetings

Communication—the ability to effectively convey ministry information and plans orally and in writing to a variety of constituents, including staff, ministry leaders, and volunteers

1. Effectively and clearly communicates the strategic and tactical objectives and plans to appropriate parties
2. Maintains a tracking system for tactical objectives/plans to limit miscommunication
3. Communicates with candor in a manner in which information can be received positively and with consistency across various functions of responsibility

Interpersonal Leadership—the ability to demonstrate interpersonal competence that builds trust and enhances interpersonal relationships in ministry

1. Listens well to others, non-defensively and with openness to hear the heart of issues
2. Maintains confidentiality
3. Communicates and conveys ideas and thoughts clearly
4. Gives and receives feedback
5. Resolves conflict biblically

Spiritual Leadership—demonstrates a commitment to spiritual growth and facilitating the spiritual growth of others; the ability to set the spiritual tone for the ministry and provide the type of leadership that inspires through consistent modeling of spiritual disciplines and practice, both public and private

1. Demonstrates Word-based faith and is faithful
2. Is sensitive and in tune with the Holy Spirit as well as his or her own interior life
3. Lives out of a clear or (growing) sense of purpose
4. Exhibits godly character as evident in his or her attitudes and actions
5. Leads with and in love—demonstrates care and compassion toward others
6. Demonstrates unity
7. Lives a biblically defined holy life
8. Demonstrates wisdom in decision making

Ministry Proficiency or Gifting–demonstrates a proficiency or gifting in a specific area of ministry, such as teaching, audio-visual, food services, health education, and so on

1. Has skills in a specific administrative or ministry area
2. Demonstrates capable gifting for service, including helps
3. Demonstrates faithfulness in serving, using skills and gifts
4. Demonstrates willingness/initiative to serve, using skills and gifts

Maturing Spiritual Walk—demonstrates spiritual growth and qualities of a maturing leader.

1. Consistently practices spiritual disciplines, such as Bible reading and prayer
2. Consistently giving of his or her time, talent, and tithe
3. Maintains a biblical lifestyle and uses the Word to guide his or her choices
4. Attends and participates in corporate prayer, worship, and Bible study

Willingness to Assume Ministry Responsibility

1. Demonstrates faithfulness to ministry
2. Conveys interest, calling, or passion to the ministry
3. Follows ministry leadership

Shows Initiative in Ministry Responsibilities

1. Demonstrates creativity and innovation in tasks assigned
2. Follows through on tasks assigned
3. Follows up with other ministry members to complete tasks
4. Provides timely updates to ministry leaders and members

Organization–demonstrates the mastery of one or more organizational leadership skills

1. Serves effectively on a ministry team
2. Follows through on projects or tasks that are started
3. Consistently demonstrates promptness to meetings and other ministry activities

GroupMe.com
- Allows ministry leaders to connect with their members through a phone application or through a simple group text message. Quicker response time than emails. Everyone will be on one accord since everyone can see everyone's response and GroupMe can cause members to be more accountable since the whole group can see their response to messages.

AnyMeeting.com
- AnyMeeting allows for group video conferences when members are not readily available to meet in person due to location or prior obligations. AnyMeeting allows for up to two-hundred people to participate. It allows for the sharing of camera video, screen video, YouTube video, share PowerPoint slides and pdf. files. Allows for polls to be taken by audience. AnyMeeting allows for a discussion mode, a question and answer mode, and a listen-only mode. AnyMeeting also allows for conference calls to be placed if everyone does not have a webcam, with a presenter access code and a guest access code.

Tableproject.org
- A social private network that operates similar to Facebook but built from the ground up for churches. Each individual church has their own free private network which allows for prayer request, event notifications, discussion boards, and etc.

E-Blasts
- Allow for announcements to be sent to the all ministry leaders and/or the whole congregation through email or text service.

Dropbox
- Dropbox allows you to share data with others for free. All you do is upload the documents, pictures, video, & etc. and all the people you want to see receive that data just logon and download the data securely.

Mediated Communication

Facebook
- Allows for the church and ministry leaders to reach people in their local area, county, state, country, and around the world. Ministry leaders can

connect and post messages about Christ, create different discussion groups, post and invite people to ministry events.

-

Twitter
- Allows ministry leaders to send short bursts of information to the website. Quick and to the point messages that plants a seed in people.

YouTube
- Allows for people outside of the church to see what the church does. Allows for people to connect with the ministry leader or church. Allows for the non-member to connect the ministry leader with a face, voice, and character.

Instagram
- Another visual tool that allows ministry leaders to connect with the online community through pictures and short video.

Ustream
- Ministry leaders can broadcast live sermons and events freely online, which can reach members that cannot make the event and even people that are not a part of the ministry or church.

Communication Strategy

SurveyMonkey
- Can conduct online and hard-copy surveys of the church and ministries. You can gauge your ministry's strength and weaknesses. You can see different views to communicate more effectively with groups in the church, nonmembers, the community, and the congregation as a whole.
- Can conduct online and hard-copy surveys of the church and ministries. You can gauge your ministry's strength and weaknesses. You can see different views to communicate more effectively with groups in the church, nonmembers, the community, and the congregation as a whole.

Imagine this leadership development process as a journey toward building a Church Full of Leaders. In this journey, there are a few key junctures at which we must stop and assess the landscape and terrain. At the heart of the Church Full of Leaders process is prayerful reflection, action, and more reflection. You started the process in prayer, immersed your leadership development process in prayer, and will need to continue to prayerfully evaluate the effectiveness of this process.

The objective of evaluation is not to deem the process a success or failure but to identify its strengths and areas for improvement. The pastor or pastoral team that approaches building a Church Full of Leaders with openness to the guidance of the Holy Spirit and a willingness to venture out into new territory and learn new things will inevitably see the power of taking time out to assess the process.

Before starting the process, you assessed the leadership needs of your church. At this point, it is critical that you evaluate the effectiveness of the leadership training. On the following page, you will find a Church Full of Leaders training feedback form that can be used as an evaluation tool. This form will help you to determine how well the instructional modules and your trainers have conveyed the lessons of the *Building a Church Full of Leaders* program. It is also useful to ascertain how pertinent these lessons were for the leaders in your church.

In addition to gathering feedback from church leaders, it is also important that the pastor and visionary leaders formally evaluate the effectiveness of the Church Full of Leaders program.

1. What worked well in the Church Full of Leaders process?

2. What did not work so well in the Church Full of Leaders process? What would you do differently?

3. In what ways are the leaders of your church:

    a. More aligned with the vision?
    b. More aware of their role as leaders?
    c. More confident in their leadership identity?
    d. More committed to the principles of transformation?
    e. More committed to serving the church?
    f. More spiritually mature?

4. What are some examples of positive leadership behaviors that you can attribute to the Church Full of Leaders emphasis?

5. In what ways are the leadership ranks expanding—where and how are more members of the congregation actively participating in the leadership and ministry processes of your church?

A Biblical Model for Organizing and Leading Transformative Ministry: An Example

EVANGELISM → WORSHIP → DISCIPLESHIP → FELLOWSHIP → SERVICE

	Evangelism	Worship	Discipleship	Fellowship	Care & Support Services	Administration	Ministry Development
	Proclaiming the Gospel	Praise, Prayer, Celebration, and Preaching	Facilitating Spiritual Growth through Teaching	Sharing, Caring and Building Relationships & Unity in the Body of Christ	Rendering Support and Helping to Meet Needs	Providing Order, Structure, and Coordination	Developing Current and New Ministries
	Clothing Drives Food Pantry/Drives Global Missions Support Nursing Home Ministry Prison Ministry	Sunday Worship Communion Baptism Music Ministry Prayer Ministries Liturgical Arts • Praise Dancers • Drama Ministry Worship Operations • Audio-Visual • Greeters • Security • Ushers	Bible Studies Children's Church Christian Living [Financial Freedom Education, Health & Wellness Education, etc.] Sunday School New Members Orientation	Marriage Ministry Men's Ministry Single's Ministry Women's Ministry Young Adult Ministry Youth Ministry	Congregational Care Funerals Support Groups Visitation Weddings	Administration • Personnel & Office Administration • IT • Communication & Media • Banquet and Food Services • King Bookstore • Transportation Ministry Operations • Building & Grounds Finance • Accounting • Payroll • Auditing	• Leadership Development & Training • School of Ministry • Ministry Engagement Process

A Biblical Model for Organizing and Leading Transformative Ministry: Template

EVANGELISM → WORSHIP → DISCIPLESHIP → FELLOWSHIP → SERVICE

Evangelism	Worship	Discipleship	Fellowship	Service		
				Care & Support Services	Administration	Ministry Development
Proclaiming the Gospel	Praise, Prayer, Celebration, and Preaching	Facilitating Spiritual Growth through Teaching	Sharing, Caring and Building Relationships & Unity in the Body of Christ	Rendering Support and Helping to Meet Needs	Providing Order, Structure, and Coordination	Developing Current and New Ministries

236

Appendix G: CFOL Ministry Engagement Volunteer Information Form

PERSONAL INFORMATION	
Last Name	First Name M.I.
Street Address	City State Zip
Gender: ❑ Female ❑ Male	Date of Birth: _____/_____/_____
Phone: _____ ❑ Landline ❑ Mobile	E-mail:
MEMBERSHIP INFORMATION	
Membership Date: _____/_____/_____	Completed Spiritul Gifts Inventory ❑ Yes ❑ No
Completed New Members Orientation ❑ Yes ❑ No	Consistent Tithing ❑ Yes ❑ No

Instructions: Please identify your skills and areas of ministry interests (check all that apply to you):

YOUR SKILLS	YOUR SKILLS	YOUR MINISTRY INTERESTS	YOUR MINISTRY INTERESTS
Evangelism/Outreach ❑ Cross-Cultural Skills ❑ Community Outreach ❑ Justice Advocacy Missions ❑ Oral Communication (Giving Presentations) ❑ Written Communi- cation **Worship** ❑ Audio-Visual ❑ Choreography ❑ Dance ❑ Instruments ❑ Media Production ❑ Singing ❑ Service Operations **Christian Education** ❑ Arts & Crafts ❑ Educational Admin. ❑ Instructional Design ❑ Teaching Adults ❑ Teaching Teens ❑ Teaching Children **Ministry Development** ❑ Leadership Dev. ❑ Planning ❑ Facilitation ❑ Survey Design & Analysis **Fellowship Ministries** ❑ Budget Tracking ❑ Logistical Skills	**Fellowship Ministries** **(cont'd)** ❑ Marketing ❑ Meeting Facilitation ❑ Program Design & Development **Admin. Ministries** ❑ Accounting ❑ Clerical ❑ Digital Media ❑ Editing ❑ Excel ❑ Graphic Design ❑ IT ❑ Marketing ❑ Power Point ❑ Word Processing **Operations** ❑ Business Dev. ❑ Commercial Driving ❑ Facility Maint. ❑ Food Services ❑ Landscaping ❑ Maintenance **General** ❑ Conflict Mediation ❑ Customer Service ❑ Entrepreneurship ❑ Event Planning ❑ Language Translation (incl. American Sign) ❑ Customer Service ❑ Entrepreneurship ❑ Event Planning	**Evangelism/Outreach** ❑ Evangelism ❑ Nursing Home ❑ Street Evangelism ❑ Visitor Follow **Worship Ministries** ❑ Audio-Visual Min. ❑ Baptism ❑ CCC Praise Ensemble ❑ CCC Musicians ❑ Children's Hallelujah Church ❑ Communion ❑ Greeters ❑ Praise Dance Ministry ❑ Prayer Ministries ❑ Security ❑ Ushers **Church Education** **Ministries** ❑ Bible Teachers (adult) ❑ Bible Teachers ❑ Leadership Dev. ❑ Vacation Bible School ❑ Teachers (children and/or teen) **Fellowship Ministries** ❑ Family Ministry ❑ Health & Wellness ❑ Marriage Ministry ❑ Men's Ministry ❑ Mother's Board ❑ New Members ❑ Singles Ministry	**Fellowship Ministries** **(cont'd)** ❑ Teen Ministry ❑ Women's Ministry ❑ Young Adult Ministry **Administration** ❑ Communication ❑ King Bookstore ❑ Office Assistance ❑ Social Media Team ❑ Transportation **Operations** ❑ Beautification (exter- nal grounds) ❑ Building & Grounds ❑ Decorating Team ❑ Event Set-Up

1. Other skills and interests not listed:

2. What do you believe your spiritual gifts are?

3. Why do you want to serve in ministry at CCC?

4. If you already know where you would like to serve, please list your ministry choices below in order of your preferences. (Three choices maximum)

1.	2.	3.

Your References: (Please list the names and contact information of two references. One can be a family member.

_____   _____

Name   Phone

_____   _____

Name   Phone

The information provided in this application is for the sole use of helping to place you into a ministry for service. Information that you have provided will be shared with discretion with auxiliary and ministry leaders you have expressed an interest in or the ministries the Ministry Engagement Team has deemed as a possible fit for service for you.

_____   _____

Signature   Date

Notes

Chapter 2: What is a Church Full of Leaders?

1. Warren Bennis and Burt Nanus. *Leaders: Strategies for Taking Charge*
    (revised edition), New York: Harper Business, 1997.

Chapter 3: The Foundation of a Church Full of Leaders

1. Herrington, Jim, R. Robert Creech, and Trisha Taylor. *The Leader's Journey:*
    Accepting the Call to Personal and Congregational Transformation.
    Hoboken: Josey-Bass, 2003.

Chapter 5: A Biblical Model for Organizing and Leading Transformative Ministry

1. *New Spirit Filled Life Bible: Kingdom Equipping Through The Power of the Word.*
    Nashville, TN: Thomas Nelson Publishers, 2002, p. 1494.

Chapter 7: Developing an Effective Ministry Structure

1. The Hartford Institute for Religion Research defines mega church as a church having sustained average weekly attendance of 2000 persons or more in its worship services. http://hirr.hartsem.edu/megachurch/definition.html

2. Keller, p 5.

3. The leadership competencies in this chapter are not exhaustive, and the aim of providing them is to provide a framework to help create a leadership infrastructure. The leader of each church will need to adapt this list for the leadership culture they are trying to cultivate. This list also does not include the "technical" or "professional" areas such as pastoral care, preaching, teaching, community economic development, etc. Any desired professional or technical competencies will need to be identified and added to position descriptions.

4. As the church grows in complexity, the need for senior leaders to become proficient in "executive" leadership functions also grows. These include financial acumen, accounting, human resource management, IT. People with these specialized skills may come forward to give of their talent and experience. In most cases the senior leader will need to hire or outsource specialized functions such as accounting, human resources management, counseling, as well as ensure professional and ethical codes and guidelines are in place for all functions.

Chapter 8: Ministry Engagement Strategy: The Pipeline for Identifying Leaders

1. *Life Application Bible.* Wheaton: Tyndale House, 1989. p. 2185

2. Pareto principle, Wikipedia

3. MeetTheNeed.org

4. Bellevue Baptist Church, based in Memphis, Tenn., once provided an online spiritual gifts assessment tool that allowed any visitor to its Web site to assess what his or he gifts were before deciding where and how they would serve.

5. Tenney, Merrill C. *Pictorial Bible Dictionary.* Grand Rapids: Zondervan,
    1963, 1964, 1967. p. 480

6. Smith, William. *Smith's Bible Dictionary.* Thomas Nelson, 1986

Chapter 10: Spiritual Formation of Leaders
1. Barton, Ruth Haley. *Sacred Rhythms: Arranging Our Lives for Spiritual Transformation.* Grand Rapids: Zondervan, 2006, p. 12
2. ibid

Chapter 12: Spiritual Disciplines for Leaders
1. Foster, Richard. *A Celebration of Discipline.* HarperSanFrancisco, 1978, p. 6
2. ibid, p. 62
3. Nouwen, Henri. *Spiritual Formation*

Chapter 14: Daily in the Word
1. BibleWorks 7th Ed.

Chapter 13: Communing with God:
1. Cornwall, Judson. *Praying the Scriptures: Communicating with God in His own Words.* Orlando, FLA: Creation House, 1979.

Chapter 16: Building Effective Ministry Teams
1. The Forming - Storming - Norming - Performing model of group development was first proposed in 1965 by Bruce Tuckman, who maintained that these phases are all necessary and inevitable in order for the team to grow, to face up to challenges, to tackle problems, to find solutions, to plan work, and to deliver results. This model has become the basis for subsequent models. Source: http://en.wikipedia.org/wiki/Tuckman_Model

Chapter 15: Sabbath Keeping: The Discipline of Rest
1 Muller, Wayne. *Sabbath: Finding Rest, Renewal, and Delight in Our Busy Lives.* New York: Bantam, 2000. p. 7
2. ibid, p. 5
3. Barton, Ruth Haley. *Sacred Rhythms: Arranging Our Lives for Spiritual Transformation.* Grand Rapids: Zondervan, 2006, pp. 134-135
4. ibid, p. 142
5. ibid, p. 142
6. ibid, p. 142
7. ibid, p. 143
8. Muller, Wayne. *Sabbath: Finding Rest, Renewal, and Delight in Our Busy Lives.* New York: Bantam, 2000. p. 8

Chapter 17: Handling Conflict in Ministry
1. © Peacemaker Ministries. Quoted with permission. Peacemaker Ministries is devoted to transforming relationships by the power of the Gospel. For more information about biblical peacemaking, visit www.Peacemaker.net.

Chapter 18: Communication for Leaders
1. http://www.statisticbrain.com/twitter-statistics/, http://www.statisticbrain.com/facebook-statistics/

At Life To Legacy, we offer quality book production, publishing, distribution, eBook conversion, and more. For more information, please visit our website at www.Life2Legacy.com or call us at (877) 267-7477.

CPSIA information can be obtained at www.ICGtesting.com
Printed in the USA
BVOW10s1441060914

365756BV00005B/9/P